THE INSECURE PASTOR

One Leader's Journey Toward Confidence

Rev. Bob Riconda

ACKNOWLEDGMENTS

Special thanks to my wife, Julie, for all the support and encouragement she gave me to write this.

Contents

Introduction

1. Why Do I Feel So Insecure?...6
2. "I Am Not The Man Everyone Thinks I Am" 14
3. Whispers From The Past 23
4. Hiding From Shame 30
5. The Curse of the American Christian Culture 38
6. Moses: Finding Strength in Your Inadequacy 46
7. Joshua: Finding Courage in Your Uncertainty 55
8. David: Finding Security in Being A Nobody 61
9. Jeremiah: Finding Confidence in Your Inexperience ...69
10. Paul: Finding Grace in Your Weakness.......................74
11. The Gospel's Answer to Insecurity 81
12. A Catalyst for Change...93

Conclusion

The Insecure Pastor

INTRODUCTION

Centuries ago Ecclesiastes warns, "of making many books there is no end, and much study is a weariness of the flesh." In the 21st century books are everywhere. Even though bookstores are closing down, Amazon has risen to superpower status online. In 2009 alone the number of books published was triple the number published in 2005. At the same time book sales are going down. Nonetheless, more and more people are writing books. Why then would I write a book?

The obvious answer is that God prompted me to.

Secondarily I am writing for pastors. Pastors live unique lives. No one really understands all that comes with pastoral ministry.

- Emotional burdens.
- Performance pressures.
- Spiritual warfare.
- Financial tensions.
- Contentious people.
- A family under scrutiny.

After thirty five years of pastoral ministry I am compelled to be a voice that empathizes and understands. It will be obvious that this book reflects my own spiritual journey and emerges from my own spiritual formation. It's not so much a 'how to' book as it is a testimony. Therefore, it is a deeply personal book. I tried to be open and honest. I really wanted to give you a glimpse into my inner life; I had to be vulnerable so you could see how a messed up young boy can be called and changed into a confident man of God.

I included Reflection Questions at the end of each chapter. I pray you will use them to start your own journey toward confidence. Maybe you'll connect. Maybe you will snatch up a truth here and there. Maybe you will be deeply moved by the Holy Spirit in a fresh way. How God uses this book in you is between Him and you. I only invite you to join in the journey...

1

Why Do I Feel So Insecure?

Success.

What does it mean to be successful?
- ✓ Brains? Check. I graduated 3rd in a high school class of 543 and graduated Bible college with Highest Honors.
- ✓ People follow you? Check. I led a youth ministry and quadrupled its size in less than 2 years.
- ✓ Popularity? Check. I was the popular teacher for a high school.
- ✓ Overcame challenges? Check. I started a church where few thought it would work.
- ✓ Longevity? Check. I led a healthy church for 18 years.
- ✓ Numbers? Check. I grew a church to over 400 in the difficult Northeast.
- ✓ Good speaker? Check. I was praised for my preaching and encouraged to go on the radio.
- ✓ Promoted? Check. I was sought after by others for denominational leadership.
- ✓ Did the impossible? Check. I married a gorgeous woman.
- ✓ Good family? Check I had three good looking, well behaved, hard working children.

In my circles, I would be considered a success!

Why do I feel so insecure?

Does success take away insecurity? Does success increase insecurity? Success and insecurity - it does not seem logical for the two to co-exist. Nonetheless, musicians, artists, ball players, business leaders, politicians, pastors, and successful leaders of all types often admit to feeling insecure. It's like we feel a great compulsion to maintain that which we've achieved. We got it and we don't want to lose it. Therefore, whether we succeed or fail, insecurity seems to lurk nearby in our hearts. I would say it is common to most people (I'd say "all" but someone would disagree and dismiss everything else I write).

Why do I feel so insecure?

It is important for me to define insecurity. Often insecurity is defined as simply a lack of safety or only a lack of self-confidence. I want to use a broader definition as I share about insecurity. It is an uncertainty about one's own value, competence, or place. In other words, it's when I feel unaccepted, unimportant, or unsafe. It's when I am afraid of rejection, failure, or uncertainty.

> **A person may display great confidence and push to be successful yet be deeply insecure because fear is what is motivating.**

A person may display great confidence and push to be successful, yet be deeply insecure because the fear of failure is what is motivating. This fear may even drive the person to manipulate others, stretch the truth, and overwork in order to appear successful or to keep the status already achieved. Maybe decisions are made on the basis of whether or not failure is a possibility.

A person may be the "life of the party," popular, and have lots of friends, yet be deeply insecure because the fear of rejection is fueling the heart. It may even push them to enable others, avoid conflict, and over-commit in order to avoid rejection and maintain the feeling of belonging. Maybe decisions are made on the basis of whether or not rejection is a possibility.

A person may be organized, well-planned, and carefully thought out, but still be deeply insecure because the fear of uncertainty is ruling. It may even cause them to isolate themselves, be dogmatic, and be rigid to avoid uncertainty and maintain control. Maybe decisions are made on the basis of whether or not uncertainty, chaos, or doubt are possible.

The Insecure Pastor

Why do I feel so insecure?

My life is not your life. Obviously we are different individuals with different backgrounds, personalities, and experiences. Nonetheless, I have a sneaky suspicion that much of what I have learned may resonate with you. Allow me to tell you my story.

I turned 50 in 2013. Whether I wanted to or not, I was driven to reflect back over my life. Books I was reading had exercises to reflect on our pasts; I skipped those parts. A conference I attended had participants make a timeline of shaping events in their lives; I glossed over it. My life coach probed into my history; I changed the subject. Finally I knew I couldn't avoid it so one cold afternoon I sat down in an empty room at our church and looked back. What God showed me was a thread, a theme that ran through my life. It probably isn't the only theme, but it was the one I needed to see right then in my life. I saw insecurity at every turn. I saw an insecure little boy struggling to be a man.

Not too long afterward my daughter and daughter-in-law thought it would be a great idea to make a photo timeline of my life for my birthday party. It was a great idea, but because I was now in a reflective frame of mind, it meant a lot more than they intended. My baby picture was adorable, but the pictures from my teen years stirred up memories I didn't want. There I was with thick rimmed glasses and a mop of black hair parted (flopped actually) to one side. I looked like a nerd ... or someone out of the movie *Argo*. Looking at that photo, I felt all the memories of insecurities rise up within me. I remember thinking, "Wow, I really was insecure. How did I get to where I am at now? How did I become the man I am today?"

To discover that answer I had to rewind my life and play some of the major scenes again in my mind.

The first scene opened in a dual level ranch house on a short side street in Old Bridge, New Jersey. A giant weeping willow adorned the side yard. Kids played in the street. Neighbors shared pools and kept an eye out for each other. It was home. It was sanctuary. It was the one place I felt safe. When neighborhood kids picked on me, I could retreat home. When bullies threatened me, I could hide there. When boredom hit, I could entertain myself there. I liked it at home. Even though dad was an alcoholic and often busy, I found great comfort in the presence of my mom and dad. Everything was safe and secure at home.

Scene one fades scene two: my junior high years at Jonas Salk Middle School. I was growing up and my younger sister joined the family, but my dad wasn't happy. Suddenly he and mom announced he was quitting his commercial artist position. They purchased a lunch wagon to sell hot dogs, sandwiches, and coffee to hungry truckers. The entire family now embarked on the challenge of a family business. It certainly provided more time together, but it was seven days a week. There was no such thing as free time or family fun time. Home became the business center. It was work, work, work.

> **"Sometimes you're the bug, sometimes you're the windshield!"**

Meanwhile junior high was a nightmare. It still stings to remember the bottle of mouthwash some classmates gave me for my birthday in the middle of math class. Or when I finally got the courage to ask a girl out, she and her girlfriends verbally mocked me in English class for having the gall to ask *her* out. Or how the kids on the bus "hired" a bully from another bus to come aboard our bus to beat me up. Or friends who always found something else better to do than be with me.

Playground taunts.

Neighborhood fights.

Busy parents.

My late friend Jim Brill would often say, "Sometimes you're the bug, sometimes you're the windshield!" I seem to recall being the bug a lot!

Scene three shifted to High School in a new neighborhood. It seemed the same things kept on happening. I became more and more isolated and shy. When I was a freshman I joined an older family friend on a cultural class trip to London. In our free time rather than spend time with the group socializing and partying, I slipped off by myself to explore the Imperial War Museum. It was quite clear to me that I was not very good at this relational stuff so better to avoid than

The Insecure Pastor

to fail ... or maybe it was better to fight. I quickly got a reputation for beating others up at the school bus stop. It wasn't that I was a bully, I just didn't want anyone bothering me plus it might make people respect or even like me. It accomplished neither.

My Life-Cam began to focus more and more at home. Being alone in my room became sanctuary for me. With my own television I could lose myself in movies and TV shows. With my toy army men I could create my own worlds. With history books and novels I explored worlds and times I never could visit. With my growing collection of board war games I conquered worlds and played to victory ... albeit solitaire. Soon pornography filled in the gap of intimacy. I was all by myself away from "dangerous people." I felt safe and secure.

Of course, I did venture outside when I had to. I did extremely well in school. Teachers liked me (or maybe pitied me). My report cards were filled with A's. I was a good compliant kid. My parents, absorbed in their own world, didn't reward me or provide praise. As a result, I often wondered why I did all I did. I wondered what my purpose, my reason for living was. "Why am I here?" My dad had no answer. Life went on.

By junior year I had developed a comfortable and seemingly reliable way of handling life. Go to school. Help with the family business. Eat dinner with my family. Lose myself in isolation. Calm. Comfortable. Safe. Every once in awhile I would feel lonely or empty, but for the most part I was happy. And then it all came crashing down in the final scene.

My isolation and ignorance kept me from seeing the corrosion in my parents' marriage. My dad's drinking had become progressively worse and my mother's resentment had grown. In a blinding flash of a few days, my mother walked out on my dad, my sister, and me. The one constant presence that gave me so much security as a child was gone. The family dinners were done. Home was no longer secure. All that I knew and all that I depended on was shattered. I felt abandoned.

There was no time to grieve. My dad needed comfort. My 12 year old sister needed someone to be strong. My parents needed someone to type up their mutual divorce agreement. As the good compliant boy I stifled my emotions and stepped forward to help, but deep within I had nothing to give. Depressed, sullen, lonely, and worn out on a summer afternoon I turned to that which often gave me some escape - my books. There on my shelf, out of place and crooked, was a book I had never read. It was a book on potential World War Three and the Second Coming of Jesus called *The Late Great Planet Earth*; I had avoided the book before because of all the religious stuff, but now something was compelling me to read it.

I gobbled up the entire book that day. By the end I knew Jesus was who I needed. Growing up I was taught I needed him for forgiveness, but there was more to Jesus I was discovering. He was the peace I longed for. He was the safety I needed. He was the purpose for life I wondered about. It was like someone had turned on a switch inside me. Everything looked different. I remembering telling someone back then that it was like I was now seeing in Technicolor ... nowadays I'd say High Definition!

I wish I could say that life with Jesus has been perfectly comfortable, safe, peaceful, and easy. In a series of rapid flashbacks I see that insecurity has tainted me over and over. I reacted defensively to people out of that insecurity. I dogmatically clamped on to certain doctrines because of insecurity. I avoided difficult people and situations out of insecurity. I made decisions for my kids out of my insecurity. I hesitated saying risky things because of insecurity. I have even done good, kind, and nice things out of heart of insecurity. I've been tangled and tripped up by insecurity more times than I want to remember. What makes it worse is that, by many standards, I was successful.

> **I've been tangled and tripped up by insecurity more times that I want to remember. What makes it worse is that, by many standards, I was successful.**

So what did I learn from rewinding my life?

Through my years of youth ministry, school teacher, church planter, lead pastor, and denominational leader God has lovingly and patiently exposed my life and then restored it to what he originally created me for. Through my 30 years of ministry I have experienced a

God far more adequate than me, yet who chose me to be his instrument. Such a feeling was something I saw emerging from the Apostle Paul's life, as well.

Paul was under such great scrutiny and criticism that I wonder how he kept from feeling insecure. When one of his churches was hearing rumors about him, he wrote, "Such is the confidence that we have through Christ toward God. Not that we are sufficient in ourselves to claim anything as coming from us, but our sufficiency is from God" (2 Corinthians 3:4-5 ESV). I believe Paul was terribly insecure in himself, but greatly secure in God. Soon after penning those words he went on to defend his ministry and then encapsulated his image of himself, "But we have this treasure in jars of clay, to show that the surpassing power belongs to God and not to us." (2 Corinthians 4:7 ESV)

Jars of clay. Simple common everyday items in every household of the time. They weren't put in a special China Cabinet to be shown off. They weren't saved for the special visitors. They weren't just found in the homes of the rich and famous. No, these jars of clay were everywhere. They may not have been expensive, but they were valuable. Nowadays coffee mugs are common place. They're everywhere and they aren't that expensive. How valuable, however, are they to the typical American in the morning? No one wants to be frantically looking for a coffee mug when they need their caffeine!

Simple.
Common.
Everywhere.
Valuable.

Therein lies Paul's security. God delights in using these coffee mugs, these simple "jars of clay."

How do we experience that security? Do feelings of insecurity ever stop? What's behind it? What does it mean to be a "jar of clay," a coffee mug?

> **Therein lies Paul's security. God delights in using these coffee mugs, these simple jars of clay.**

I hope my journey will help answer these questions and more for you.

FOR YOUR OWN REFLECTION:

- On a large poster board draw a line across the widest part; this will represent the timeline of your life. Include childhood, adolescence, and adulthood.

- Using Post-It Notes, write down significant events that happened in your life. Use one color for positive and another for negative.

- Arrange them in order on your timeline.

- Prayerfully reflect over the events and ask the Holy Spirit to illuminate your memory and show patterns.

- Write down your observations and lessons.

2

"I Am Not The Man Everyone Thinks I Am"

When I was studying for the ministry at Philadelphia College of the Bible it all seemed much easier. Right and wrong. Black and white. In the classroom ministry seemed clinical and formulaic. Live right, do right. A few professors tried to shake up our thinking. One shared privately with me what happened to him in one of his pastorates when we were discussing qualifications for church leadership. He was interviewing a man to serve as an elder in his church. He was a faithful and devoted husband and father, was well thought of by his neighbors and co-workers, and was solid in his faith. A no brainer ... until he humbly shared that he had been married years before. His first wife left him right after the ceremony before ever consummating the marriage and ran off to become a nun. My professor looked at me, "So what do you do?"

Maybe it was youthful naiveté or idealism, but it was most likely faulty thinking that life can be reduced to a simple formula: FAITH + OBEDIENCE = COMFORTABLE LIFE. I certainly didn't teach that. I know I counseled people toward intimacy with Jesus and not toward getting His blessings here and now. I told people that there were no guaranteed promises of a comfortable blessed prosperous life this side of heaven. In hindsight, however, there was a misplaced belief in my heart. Deep within I believed I will live right and everything will turn out right. It might not be true for everyone else, but I get it. That's right, I will show everyone how it's done. And all looked well until 2009.

That year I was transitioning out of the beloved church I started to go on denominational staff. I was not really in touch with the grief I was feeling but I knew something was going on. Sitting on the rocks overlooking the Aegean in Greece I wrote in my journal:

Monday, September 14

I want a new work of mercy done in me. I'm embarrassed by the lack of desire for You I have. I have been comfortable with my knowledge of you ... like that's enough. I sense there is more and I do want to know, to go deeper. I haven't lost my love for You, I'm just not increasing it. Wow, how complacent and lazy I've become. Stir my heart, Lord. Light the fire again. I want you and nothing else.

As I sat there on the rocks of Nafplio I remember hearing a loud boom sound. I couldn't see where it was coming from. The waves were hitting the rocks but it didn't seem violent enough to warrant the sound. The rocks looked strong, solid, even majestic; they were standing their ground against the waves. But when the tide lowered I saw where the sound was coming from. Underneath the rocks a deep swath had been carved by the waves below water level and out of sight. These solid rocks were actually compromised by erosion. Soon they would collapse due to that erosion. At that moment I sensed that was me. I looked strong and solid outwardly, but inwardly something was eroding. I wrote the next day:

Tuesday, September 15

I'm not adequate for the task before me for sure. So I must be close to You, I must abide in You. I must draw strength from You. Be my center, the wind in my sails, the rudder of my life. These last few years have been rough for my relationship with You. Cynicism and complacency have eroded my life, I cannot and will not rely on yesterday's lessons or growth or relationship. I want You today. All of you, nothing more nothing less.

A month later as I began my new ministry I had an emotional breakdown. Panic attacks, insomnia, anxiety, depression overwhelmed me and I was a mess. I couldn't control my own self. I feared I was going crazy. I was afraid I was letting down my wife and my new boss. At the same time my daughter was arrested at college for admitting suicidal ideation and I was diagnosed with a stomach disorder that radically changed my diet. I couldn't eat for comfort. I couldn't lose myself in exciting movies or TV shows (because they'd trigger anxiety). I couldn't sleep. My image of a perfect family was shattered. My image of being a strong man was stripped away. I was broken, weak, powerless. No one could help. Nothing made me feel better. All I had was God ... so I had no choice but pursue Him.

Without knowing it I had created a persona, an image of myself, of family, of ministry that I could control. I now see control as an illusion.

As I reread my journal I see this crisis as answered prayer from the previous month. Through that six month episode I learned a great many truths and deepened my relationship with God. Without knowing it I had created a persona, an image of myself, of family, of ministry that I could control. I now see control as an illusion. I am not now nor can I ever really be in control. As Tim Chester says, "God is great so I don't have to be in control."[1]

It often takes a tsunami to overwhelm the comfortable illusion of control we've built:
- Your spouse admits having an affair.
- Your teenage daughter gets pregnant.
- The church splits.
- The principal calls for a meeting about your son.
- A best friend betrays you.
- The biopsy comes back malignant.
- The treasurer has been embezzling money from the church.
- The panic attacks don't get any better.
- Depression.

Personal and family problems foster insecurity because they highlight weakness to ourselves. Our porcelain images are shattered. Our safe houses are invaded. Our foundation is eroded. We can no longer deny it. We see our own failures. We are really not the persons we thought we were.

And that may not be bad.

During the six months of my emotional turmoil I visited one doctor who used a machine to analyze brain waves and my brain's health. In my initial visits he told me that my brain showed signs of being worn out by anxiety. I asked, "For how long, 18 months?" I had figured that the 18 month pastoral transition was behind this. His reply shocked me, 'No, more like 18 years." He did not know that that was exactly how long I served as a lead pastor.

There is tremendous stress and anxiety that a pastor goes through. There are layers of pressure upon a pastor's soul that differ from other vocations. Years ago I was told that the emotional energy used in a 30 minute sermon is the equivalent of 8 hours of hard labor. Besides that there is the inner burden of caring for a large group of people - it's like having dozens of children that you worry about. Late night phone calls. Constant interruptions. Persistent complaints. Unfair behavioral expectations that are placed on the pastor's family, and having to handle the fallout of that. What about spiritual warfare? Would not the enemy want to take out the leaders of God's army? The emotional, spiritual, and physical pounding is relentless upon a pastor. No one really understands, there's no comparison.

> **I wonder if some of the high standard that American evangelicalism has for pastors have done a disservice to our hearts.**

I wonder if some of the high standards that American evangelicalism has for pastors have done a disservice to our hearts. I am not saying remove all the standards, but I am questioning the environment that judgmentalism and legalism created. Take for example, the pastor who is having trouble with one of his children. Since he would lose his job if it came out, he hides, lives in insecurity that someone will find out, and puts on a front that everything is alright. The stigma of marital trouble, mental illness, rebellious teens, and divorce breeds insecurity. No one admits they have a problem. No one talks about it. Instead we all think to ourselves, "What am I doing wrong? What's wrong with me?"

The Insecure Pastor

In the last few years, I have known and have talked to: a pastor whose wife had a mental illness divorced and left him for another man; a pastor struggling with his own emotional issues divorced his wife and left the ministry; two pastors who are taking medication for depression, a associate pastor whose wife had an affair, a youth pastor who was arrested for soliciting a prostitute; an associate pastor whose wife has a mental illness but doesn't want to help herself nor live with him; a church planter who resigned because his wife left with the kids for no apparent reason; and three pastors who have a child who wants nothing to do with God. Many of these situations were happening for some time but no one knew because frankly we just don't talk about these kinds of issues.

> **No amount of self-effort or religious standards or behavioral modification is going to reverse the fact that we are all broken, including us pastors.**

There's a little Chinese takeout place in my town that has a large fish tank. While waiting for my order I can watch beautiful fish swimming peacefully about. It's actually really nice. It wouldn't, however, be appetizing if that aquarium was filled with fish biting and shredding each other like piranhas. Blood would cloud the water and fish parts would float by. My Sesame Chicken would not seem so appealing anymore! No, we want our fish to look happy and peaceful. In the same way, we want our pastor and family to look right, to act right, to have it all together.

It is this mindset that increases our insecurity as pastors. Maybe because it makes us feel like we are living a lie. Maybe because we are afraid of being labeled frauds, phonies, or hypocrites. We have been put on a pedestal to be admired and gawked at but never exposed as weak and in need of grace just like everyone else. For example, I remember numerous times people would talk to me after a service, maybe ask me to pray for them, and say, "I know you're a godly and prayerful man." I would nod and politely thank them. In my mind, however, "Wait! How do you know that? I don't always feel too godly. And honestly if I don't pray in the next few minutes for you, I will probably forget this week." Other times, I'd wonder, "Is that who you really think I am or who you expect me to be?"

Sometimes this reinforces our own pride and we believe our self created illusions, but reality will soon expose us. People don't see us when we yell at our kids, wish bad on people, curse in our heads, glance at porn, waste time, act selfishly with our wives, or worry about life and the church. They don't see us when we are afraid and anxious. They don't know how we struggle with the fear of man, the fear of failure, or the fear of an uncertain future. And those fears, those anxieties are expressions of our insecurity. We might be found out because we are not who people think we are.

> **This is not to say that we dismiss our hang ups and minimize our sins. Nor do I suggest that we use "being real" as an excuse to mistreat people or overburden them with our emotions.**

I don't think the Apostle Paul worried about being found out. After admitting the stresses and anxiety of his life and ministry he pleads with one of his churches, "We have spoken freely to you, Corinthians; our heart is wide open. You are not restricted by us, but you are restricted in your own affections. In return (I speak as to children) widen your hearts also." (2 Corinthians 6:11-13 ESV) I have been real with you. I have been open and honest. I have not hid my weakness or my struggles. He's trying to create an environment of genuineness, vulnerability, and transparency.

We would do much better to create this kind of environment for ourselves, our families, and our churches. It's time we face the reality of, to use a theological term, total depravity. No amount of self effort or holding to religious standards or behavioral modification or successful ministry is going to reverse the fact that we are all broken, including us pastors. That total depravity has affected us physically (sickness), mentally (mental illness), emotionally (grief), socially (broken relationships) and spiritually (separation from God). Like a copy of a copy, the human race is feeling the effects of the Fall generation to generation. We as pastors are not exempt so why fake it.

Instead I suggest we learn to admit our brokenness with vulnerability and transparency so that God's grace can be shown.

> But we have this treasure in jars of clay, to show that the surpassing power belongs to God and not to us. (2 Corinthians 4:7 ESV)

For consider your calling, brothers: not many of you were wise according to worldly standards, not many were powerful, not many were of noble birth. But God chose what is foolish in the world to shame the wise; God chose what is weak in the world to shame the strong; God chose what is low and despised in the world, even things that are not, to bring to nothing things that are, so that no human being might boast in the presence of God. (1 Corinthians 1:26-29 ESV)

I recall recently hearing someone say that "the saints were not nice guys." A scanning of a few of the major names in the Bible might lead us that way:
- Noah got drunk and sprawled out naked. (Genesis 9:21)
- Abraham & Sarah tried to fulfill God's promise in their own way and time. (Genesis 16)
- Isaac lied about Rebekkah to protect his own butt. (Genesis 26)
- Jacob lied to his father so he could get the money. (Genesis 27)
- Judah had sex with a prostitute who happened to be his daughter-in-law. (Genesis 38)
- Moses murdered an Egyptian. (Exodus 2:11-15)
- Joshua didn't pray before making a crucial alliance. (Joshua 9)
- Samuel's sons were mean, profane, deceitful leaders. (1 Samuel 8)
- David had an affair and had someone killed to cover it up. (2 Samuel 11)
- Peter was rebuked for prejudice. (Galatians 2:11-14)
- Paul couldn't work with everyone. (Acts 15:36-41)

There are so many more examples of pre and post Cross saints who didn't have it all together, whose families were a mess, whose children didn't follow God, and who didn't get along with people. I doubt any would be allowed to pastor American churches today!

This is not to say that we dismiss our hang ups and minimize our sins. Nor do I suggest that we use "being real" as an excuse to mistreat people or overburden them with our emotions. Rather we are to live in the light and not hide behind a religious veneer. As my wife counsels, "There is a time and a place." Now is not always the right time nor is everywhere the right place. There is a place for discretion.

There are tangible benefits from leading with vulnerability and transparency. After preaching one week and admitting my own faults, one woman told me, "Thank you for sharing that. You make the Christian life attainable." After sharing my emotional breakdown in a message on 2 Corinthians 1, a line of people came up to me to hug me, "Thank you for making me feel like I am not alone." Recently a pastor sent me a long text venting over a situation in his church. At the same time I was on the phone with another pastor who was doing the same. Both were angry, raw, and not very nice. When they apologized for talking to me that way, I said, "That's why I am here. I don't think bad of you. I've been there, I understand." These men can serve with confidence because it's safe to not be perfect. Finally I think it lowers anxiety and consequently insecurity because you have nothing to hide.

What was broken has been mended, mended by the King of love.
King of glory, King of love, every throne established in fear is toppled in love.
- lyrics by Jamie Fitt

FOR YOUR OWN REFLECTION:

1. What difference have you seen between those who come clean with their issues and those who keep them to themselves?

2. Why might people be fearful of sharing their private issues with you?

3. What is something about yourself that you have never told anyone? Why not?

4. Who are those that you can confide in?

5. What would happen if you told someone everything about yourself?

---

[1] - Chester, T. (2010). *You can change: God's transforming power for our sinful behavior and negative emotions.* Wheaton, IL: Crossway.

3

Whispers From The Past

As a youngster the 1973 "made for TV" movie called *Don't Be Afraid of the Dark* brought shivers to me. The story involves small dwarf-like creatures which infest the basement of an old house and harass a woman who has just moved in with her husband. What freaked me out was the way the creatures communicated with each other; they spoke in eerie whispers, taunting, warning, and planning.

"Don't hurt her...not yet."
"I want to. "
"Wait until tomorrow."
"Let me just scare her."
"Alright. Then scare her!"

I was afraid that conniving little creatures were lurking in my house. They were whispering plans to hurt me when the lights turned off.

As an adult I hear whispers. Since they are not shouts or loud voices, I am not always aware of them, but they echo through my subconscious. They are insidious and destructive. They undermine my confidence and fuel insecurity. These voices also plot my demise. They are whispers from my past. Words others have spoken to me. Words I have repeated to myself. These "voices" from our past feed insecurity.

For the initial years of my marriage I acted more out of insecurity than love with my wife. I did what she wanted not because I loved her, but because I was afraid she might leave me like my mom left my dad. Whispers from my junior high years had me believing I was neither loveable or desirable. It didn't matter how many times my wife told me otherwise. I didn't believe her because the whispers had been with me much longer ... and I wasn't aware of them.

Recently I noticed I am still surprised when people actually want to spend time with me, not as pastor, not as co-worker, but as

Bob. Why? Because there is still a residue left by those whispers. Lies that I am not likeable or worth being a friend with.

I know I am not the only one. In 30 years of ministry I have heard the whispers in other's lives, too. "I am clumsy." "You will never be good at anything." "I am just not a good student; I am dumb." "I have to be perfect." "You're meaningless." "Worthless." Some of the whispers are actual words spoken to us. There are misguided parents who never give praise, but always found reason for criticism. The older sibling who put you down constantly. The teacher who embarrassed you in front of the entire class. The angry dad who yelled obscenities and called you names. The manipulative mom who made you feel guilty simply by the way she said things. The co-workers who talked behind your back.

    Humiliated.

        Corrected.

            Mocked.

                Cut.

                    Abused.

These are whispers of little creatures out to destroy us.

Often times, it's not words, but our interpretations of others' actions. A parent who is absent may communicate non-verbally to a child that he or she is not worthy of their presence or time. Take for example, those who are adopted.

> "I can't speak for all adult adoptees but I can say—after interviewing several of them over the years—that many of us have trouble feeling completely comfortable wherever we are—no matter how welcomed we may be. At times our discomfort can manifest in distancing, indifference, or even rudeness, but we usually don't intend to insult anybody. We just seem to have an internalized nomadic notion that we don't belong anywhere in particular. Even when we do settle somewhere we often work our asses off to prove our worthiness—just in case anyone gets any ideas about putting us back up for adoption." [1]

My friends never told me I was not good enough to be their friend, but they often had "other things" to do rather than spend time with me. Many times it was right before we were supposed to meet or they just never showed up. I interpreted their behavior to mean I was not good or likeable enough to be their friend. Sometimes our interpretations are right, sometimes not. I found out years later they were doing drugs so it wasn't about me. Even so, the whispers took root and affected me for years. Whether or not our interpretations are accurate does not change the whispers. There are there and they are real to us.

In the church I led for 18 years we had times at the end of our Sunday gatherings where we prayed for the sick. People were invited to come forward and the elders and pastors would sit with them, lay hands on them, and pray for them. One Sunday a young couple came forward with marital troubles. When we were praying for them, I was impressed to pray that the husband would know how valuable he was; I then spoke of the Father's tender heart toward him and how he wanted to be the dad he never had. It had little to do with their request, but it had everything to do with their struggles. When I finished, they were both sobbing; they looked up and he said, "No one has ever said that to me before. How did you know?" The whispers of the past were exposed and a new freedom was begun for him and his wife.

> **There is a lie propagated to all youngsters of my generation, "sticks and stones may break my bones, but words will never hurt me."**

Decades ago family counselors Drs. Gary Smalley and John Trent wrote a book called *The Blessing*.[2] Their thesis is that we all have a powerful need to know that someone in this world loves us and accepts us unconditionally. This especially is true in relationship to our parents. Without their 'blessing' we often are angry and driven, or detached and empty. It also may cause us miss out on intimacy and closeness in other key relationships - between brothers and sisters, husbands and wives, or within our faith community. Without the positive voice of a "parental blessing," the insidious whispers rule our hearts.

The Insecure Pastor

There is a lie propagated to all youngsters of my generation, "Sticks and stones may break my bones, but words will never hurt me." On the contrary, words carry enormous power. Proverbs 18:21 puts it, "Death and life are in the power of the tongue." Words can start wars and bring peace. Words start a marriage and end it. Whether it's praise, criticism, deception, gossip, slander, comfort, or encouragement, we do it all with words. Now, what happens when the negative words spoken to us (or by us) entrench themselves in our minds? In the ensuing years they echo through our psyches as whispers. Those whispers often breed insecurity because they're not founded on current reality, but on the words of years before.

They can, and often do, shape us. Many people either end up living in ways to prove those whispers are not true or others resign to live as though the whispers are true. The whisper of "you're worthless" can make someone work relentlessly and incessantly. Maybe they cannot slow down and enjoy God's gift of Sabbath. Maybe they cannot say "No" to anyone who wants to meet. Maybe they have to refine their sermon over and over. Maybe they work on their vacation. Maybe they get stubbornly defensive when someone criticizes or disagrees. Maybe they collapse into anxiety when things seem to go wrong. They cannot and will not fail! Because if they do, then it means those whispers are true. So they spin the wheel of perfection striving for success to prove their worth.

Or take it the other direction. Maybe they refuse to pursue any big dreams. Maybe they're always settling for less. Maybe they don't take risks or push themselves. Maybe they play it safe all the time. Maybe they don't challenge people. Maybe they never fight back. Maybe they lose themselves in a secret comfort or sin. They believe they're already failures so what's the use? The whispers are true so they just want to get by without more pain.

A few weeks after I turned 30 my first youth pastor asked me, "Do you feel like an adult yet?" It was an insightful question. I was thirty years old, yet I still didn't feel like an adult. Deep within I still felt like a little boy. Even though I had successfully planted a church I still doubted my competence in ministry. Even though I had three children and was married for 9 years I still wondered if I was qualified to be a husband, a dad, a leader. Whispers. What do I think I am doing? Wasn't I still a kid?

In Luke 19 Jesus is on his way to Jerusalem. It will be his penultimate visit; he will ride in as a triumphant king. Multitudes will wave palms and praise him. Before he gets there, however, he passes through the town of Jericho. Crowds have gathered there to see him. One man in particular has a rough time in the crowd. Zacchaeus is a tax collector. No one likes having him around because, as far as the Jews are concerned, he works for their enemies and skims off their taxes for his own benefit. They won't let him through. To make matters worse, he's short and can't see over the crowd. So he runs ahead, climbs a sycamore tree, and waits for Jesus to walk by. And when Jesus came to the place, he looked up and said to him, "Zacchaeus, hurry and come down, for I must stay at your house today." (Luke 19:5 ESV) Simple words, but loaded with life. Filled with power to silence whispers. *No wonder Jesus was so controversial*

Jesus singled out the person who was most insecure. He was looked down upon in all respects. He was maligned for his job. He was mistrusted for his cheating ways. He was frowned upon by the religious and the commoner. He probably lived in anxiety and fear wondering if the some zealot would kill him or the Romans would discover his skimming. Yet Jesus gives no rebuke, no criticism, no correction. Instead he offers what Zacchaeus has the least of - unconditional acceptance. The famous Jesus *wants* to spend time with him. With those words Jesus gives life to someone deadened by the whispers of others.

This is what the truth of the gospel does for us if we let it. The only way to counteract the effects of the whispers is to hear the voice of Jesus. He tells us what the Father thinks of us. In Luke 15 Jesus is confronted by the religious people of his day. They were upset with him for hanging out with those who aren't religious, called sinners. The prevalent religious thought in that time was basically: follow the rules, do the rituals, be good, and earn the right to be with God. At that time there was a clear barrier between the religious and the sinners. Pharisaic regulations were explicit, "entrust no money to him, take no testimony from him, trust him with no secret, do not appoint him guardian of an orphan, do not make him custodian of charitable funds, do not accompany him on a journey." [3] Jesus told a trilogy of stories to make a point to the religious people about what God is really like. The finale' or the pinnacle is the story we know today as the Parable of the Prodigal Son. It is that story in which Jesus highlights God as a father who does not exclude either brother, the bad one or the good one, the prodigal one or the compliant one. Instead, the father initiates and reaches out with acceptance, value, and provision for both.

Think of the whispers that might have been echoing in the prodigal son's head - "failure," "worthless," "unwanted," "a slave with pigs."

Also think of the whispers that might have been echoing in the older brother's head - "work hard," "do your duty," "make sure to obey or else," "better be good."

In both cases the father counteracts those whispers. Obviously for the younger son, he throws a party and restores his dignity and identity as a beloved son. For the older he reminds him of truth, "Son, you are always with me, and all that is mine is yours." (Luke 15:31). No reason to work, just be with me. No reason to prove yourself, I already accept you. No reason to try to earn my blessing, it is yours for the asking. Don't believe the lies. Believe my truth.

When you see people whispering nearby, what do you think? They're keeping something from you? They're talking about you? They're saying things that shouldn't be heard? Rarely do we think it's something positive. Whispering gives off negative vibes. Our instinct is to think it's something bad or, at best, questionable. Whispers feed insecurity. The only way to uncover the whispers is to first expose them. Once we recognize the whispers and identify them, then we can counteract them with something more powerful - the Words of Jesus.

This is why counseling is so important. For me - it has been the place to identify the whispers. I am still learning to recognize the voice of Jesus.

FOR YOUR OWN REFLECTION:

Sometimes we have a hard time hearing the whispers in our subconscious. Ask the Holy Spirit to help you remember and bring to your mind what needs to be uncovered today.

1. What words did your parents use to describe you?

2. How did you interpret their actions toward you?

3. What other significant people spoke to you or to others about you? What did they say?

4. What lie do you tell yourself about what is needed to be successful in ministry?

5. What thoughts come to your mind when you face failure, rejection, or uncertainty?

---

[1] - Stephen J Betchen D.S.W., (April 11, 2011) "Why Adoptees Need to Find Their Biological Parents," *Psychology Today*

[2] - Trent, J., & Smalley, G. (2011). *The Blessing: giving the gift of unconditional love and acceptance.* Nashville: Thomas Nelson.

[3] - Barclay, W. (1975). *The Gospel of Luke.* Philadelphia, PA; Westminster Press, pg. 199.

4

Hiding From Shame

Shame, n. - a painful feeling of humiliation or distress caused by the consciousness of wrong or foolish behavior. - Webster's Dictionary

In 2009 friends of ours gave us a little Havanese puppy from their new litter. At first we didn't want a dog in the house, but who can turn down such a wonderful gift? We named him Astro and he has been a part of our family since then. He has been a delightful addition. Not only is he affectionate, but watching him relate to us as masters has shed light on our relationship with God. For example, he is usually very well behaved and obedient. But every once in awhile we see him sitting in the corner with his head down. He won't look at us or even wag his tail. Sure enough, that means he got into the garbage and made a mess. In some canine way, he feels shame and is hiding. That is very reminiscent of another story. "And they heard the sound of the Lord God walking in the garden in the cool of the day, and the man and his wife hid themselves from the presence of the Lord God among the trees of the garden." (Genesis 3:8 ESV). After choosing their way rather than God's, Adam and Eve were filled with shame and hid from God. They knew that what they did was wrong. They knew something was now broken in their relationship with God. Their response, like Astro's, was to hide.

We are all broken, imperfect, and tainted with sin. No one has it all together. No one has arrived. The Apostle Paul admitted, "Not that I have already obtained this or am already perfect, but I press on to make it my own, because Christ Jesus has made me his own." (Philippians 3:12 ESV). Even the great saints of the Bible were broken and flawed. From Noah to Peter we do not read of spiritual superheroes who always rise to the occasion and never do anything wrong. Instead God's hall of fame is filled with flawed men and women who, even when they loved Him, made poor choices and blew it.

We all face the specter of some standard to live up to. It comes in various forms; the expectations of our parents, the requirements of a career, the non-verbal 'rules' of our social circle, the mandates of societal norms, or the standards of religion and faith. It might actually be the demands we place on ourselves because we have listened to whispers from our past. Whatever standard it is, when we don't live up to it, we feel shame or guilt.

Guilt and shame are relatives in the family tree of insecurity. Though the distinction is not always clear, I explain it like this. Guilt is often associated with the clear breaking of rules; it reflects on what I do and deals with behavior -- "I feel guilty because I lied about who started the fight." Shame, on the other hand, is associated with a perceived failure to live up to some image or picture; it reflects on who I am and deals with identity --- "I am a bad son because I didn't call my mom every week from college." Moreover it is true that patterns of guilt inducing behavior cause shameful views of oneself. Both bring painful feelings of humiliation or distress.

> *Guilt and shame are relatives in the family tree of insecurity.*

No one likes those painful feeling of humiliation or distress. We want them to go away so we hide. And, boy, do we know how to hide. From the Garden onward we have become very proficient at hiding. After examining my experience with myself and others, I have summarized the ways we hide into three categories: we ignore, we excuse, we blame.

- **WE IGNORE:** We don't want to face our failures so we go to great efforts to avoid or ignore them. We may get busy packing our schedules or become workaholics. We may go to unhealthy extremes with hobbies, sports, exercise. We may indulge in numbing agents of alcohol, drugs, media, entertainment. We may cover our shortcomings with religious activity, altruistic service, or more ministry. We are trying to "medicate" ourselves so we don't *feel* shame. All the while we are actually keeping the Father at a distance. Our relationship with God becomes academic, sterile, or just plain dull. Our intimacy with Him suffers because we have not let Him into the area of our lives where shame exists. When the Spirit nudges us to go there, we respond with "I'm fine" or "Others have bigger issues," and continue doing more for God.

- **WE EXCUSE:** We don't want to face our failures so we try to weasel out by finding loopholes and excuses. We may change the rules by lowering the standards or by negating them. What was wrong before might no longer be wrong. We may excuse ourselves because of sickness, lack of sleep, crying kids, or long hours at work. Basically the rules don't apply to me because I am different. "I was tired." This leads some to avoid any chance of failure by staying away from situations in which they could fail; they stick to that which they are good or competent at. As a result, our faith suffers. We miss out on seeing God's power work; instead, we only see our own power work.

- **WE BLAME:** Rather than facing our failures we focus on others'. We may blame the government, the corporations, the church, or the economy. We may blame those close to us - parents, spouse, friends, co-workers, etc... As a result, we may pull away from those who remind us of our failure. Intimacy is lost. In extreme cases, friendships end, marriages broken, and churches split. We may even blame God (but then some shame may keep us from even admitting that!). Because of the intense power of shame we cannot accept responsibility for anything we do that would make us feel that shame again. We will not see our own faults. Instead we are oversensitive and defensive. We take on a victim identity. We may have been wounded; we may have been victimized, but now we are victims all the time, everywhere, with everyone. As a result, our love suffers. We end up running from deep relationships.

All of our attempts at hiding do not remove shame. They actually make it worse by strengthening shame's grip on us. Shame, in turn, reinforces insecurity. This continues in an unending loop. Sin (whether real or perceived) leads to shame leads to hiding which leads to more sin and more shame, etc....

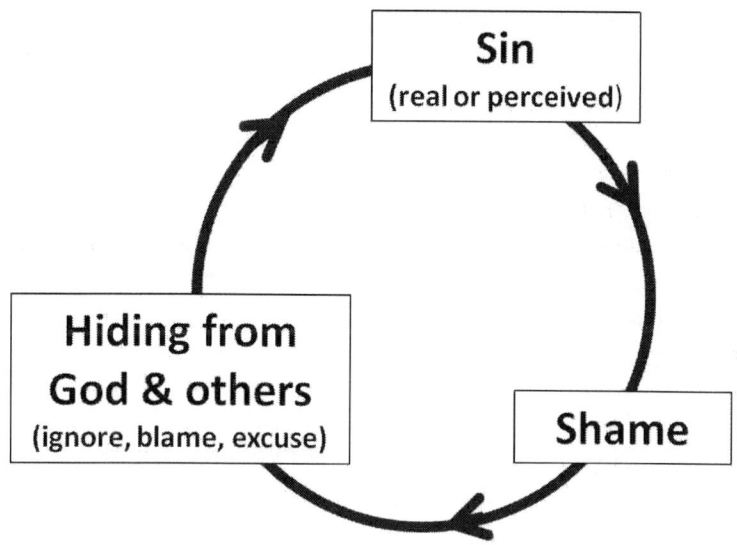

I saw this in one young couple who was struggling in their marriage. Neither was experiencing much intimacy with the other. Instead they each felt distant from the other, as though a wall were between them. This often led to conflicts and hurt feelings. It soon came out in our conversations that they had had pre-marital sex. They both had deeply held convictions about saving themselves for marriage, but they succumbed to temptation a few months before the wedding. Not only was I the first person they had told, but they had never talked about it themselves. After not berating them, but reminding them of the Cross, I encouraged them to talk with each other about it and apologize to each other. Their confession brought forgiveness, a lifting of shame, and a new closeness in their marriage as they stopped hiding.

I also saw this with a woman who struggled with overeating. She had used food for years as a comfort to life's troubles. The god of food was not kind to her body. She soon gained lots of weight. Instead of her appearance motivating her to stop eating, it actually inflamed it. Looking at her body made her feel shameful (especially since positive body image was a value passed on by her family). She would try to numb that feeling in the only way she knew how - eating. Round and round she would go.

This was also true in my own life. Lustful thoughts, fantasies, and glimpses at pornography incited me to be selfish in my marriage. I felt ashamed at violating my marriage vows. Nonetheless, I would not admit my thoughts or actions, but instead became irritable and demanding. As you can imagine that spirit certainly did not do anything to bring closeness in my relationship; on the contrary, it actually brought resentment and distance.

> **Shame keeps us in bondage through secrets.**

Sometimes shame is not rooted in our own sin, but in the sin of others. Men and women who tragically experienced childhood sexual abuse are usually inundated with shame. It will warp their identity, taint their view of sexuality, or form lifelong self-protective habits. One may be hyper-vigilant and controlling. Another may throw himself or herself into sexual fetishes or perversions, often it is kept in secret because "ministers don't struggle with those things." Compounding this is the specter of family secrets. Whether we grew up in a dysfunctional family system or in a pastor's family where we couldn't admit problems because "daddy might lose his job," shame keeps us in bondage through secrets.

Hiding from shame distances us from God and from people. Intimacy is ruined. We walk around insecure, afraid we'll be found out. There has to be a better way. Maybe that's the way Paul felt before writing, "But I need something more! For if I know the law but still can't keep it, and if the power of sin within me keeps sabotaging my best intentions, I obviously need help! I realize that I don't have what it takes. I can will it, but I can't do it. I decide to do good, but I don't really do it; I decide not to do bad, but then I do it anyway. My decisions, such as they are, don't result in actions. Something has gone wrong deep within me and gets the better of me every time. It happens so regularly that it's predictable. The moment I decide to do good, sin is there to trip me up. I truly delight in God's commands, but it's pretty obvious that not all of me joins in that delight. Parts of me covertly rebel, and just when I least expect it, they take charge. I've tried everything and nothing helps. I'm at the end of my rope. Is there no one who can do anything for me?" (Romans 7:17-24 MSG) He has obviously fallen short of a standard, God's law. Shame and guilt, powerlessness and weakness cannot be escaped. Rather than ignore, excuse, or blame, Paul admits his failure and looks for help.

As you may have expected Paul's help will come from Jesus. It is how that helps comes that I find relevant to dealing with insecurity. The first thing he says about this help is, "There is therefore now no condemnation for those who are in Christ Jesus." (Romans 8:1 ESV). No judgment, no punishment, no separation, no abandonment, no rejection. It reminds me of what one of the facilitators of a recent Pastors' Prayer Retreat shared, "God is not mad at you." For some of the pastors there, these were life giving words. They shared with me how often they feel like they're letting God down, that they're not good enough to be pastors, that they must have messed up somewhere. Their shortcomings, whether legitimate or exaggerated, were producing shame.

Over my years in ministry people have come into my office and shared something they never told anyone else. They usually warn me ahead of time, shift around, glance away, and finally lean forward to speak. Sexual abuse, pornography, adultery, murder, stealing, homosexuality, drug abuse, violence, etc.... I always made it my habit to never act shocked. I would pray, "Lord, enable me to extend grace by my verbal and non-verbal reactions." God is not shocked by our secrets, our sins, or our shame.

There is a great transition between Romans 7 and 8. In chapter 7 Paul uses the personal pronoun "I" twenty-four times; in chapter 8 he uses the word "Spirit" 18 times. I and my hiding cannot deal with shame, God and his Spirit can. God's Spirit frees us from guilt & shame. There is no condemnation. This is powerful when we put it in context. Paul was a mess, entangled in his own inadequacies and failures. He tried and tried and tried and still ended up failing, unable to break the power of the sin nature in his daily life. It's like those of us who cry out:

"My church never grows; I am just a bad leader."
"I ruined my marriage. What's the use of going on."

"I'm a loser; God can't use me."
"I fell again; I guess I'm just not a good Christian."
"I just can't let others see me like this; I'm ashamed."
"Why would God want me back?"

Our self-condemning thoughts (whispers) only bring guilt and shame, insecurity and fear. Meanwhile, the Spirit is saying we're not condemned, we're not hopeless cases, we're not losers.

Our hearts are complex and mysterious to the point that figuring ourselves out is like an endless walk through a maze or navigating an ever changing arena in *Hunger Games*. What we do to help ourselves doesn't. Instead it feeds what we want less of - insecurity. We attempt to be good people by relying upon our own strength. We push ourselves to win God's approval or our parents or our own. Naturally when we fail, we don't like it because it exposes us as weak and needy. We feel shame, hide, and become more insecure at our inability. Like children yearning for our parents' approval we strive and try harder, hoping that finally God will smile at us and pat us on the back for all the hard work we've done. But the Spirit frees us from endless pursuits and fruitless attempts to please God. Performance doesn't deal with shame, the Spirit does.

He does so when we admit our failure, when we confess our sins, when we reveal our secrets, when we accept our imperfection, when we depend on Him. It may be humbling. It may be threatening and scary. Everything within us may fight against such a surrender. But what do we have to lose? There isn't any condemnation. He already knows you're a mess and He's not mad at you.

> *"Behold, I am laying in Zion a stone of stumbling, and a rock of offense; and whoever believes in him will not be put to shame."*
> *- Romans 9:33 ESV*

FOR YOUR OWN REFLECTION:

1. How do you distinguish between shame and guilt in your own life?

2. Which of the three ways do you tend to use to hide - excuse, ignore, blame?

3. In any society or culture there are certain stigmas or taboos (e.g., being sexually abused, same sex attraction, mental illness, demonic oppression, etc...) which when admitted bring shame upon an individual or a family. Which might you or your family be facing?

4. If shame deals more with identity ("I am a _____"), then how might confession clarify who you are?

5. What secrets are you keeping that shape how you really see yourself?

5

The Curse of the American Christian Culture

When I was a high school teacher one of my freshman students heard I enjoyed Star Trek. He and his parents surprised me by getting tickets to the upcoming Star Trek Convention in Philadelphia. It was a big event like today's Comic-Con Conventions so I was excited to go to my first one. It was everything Star Trek. There were booths for products, rooms for presentations and workshops, meeting areas for local clubs. There were interviews, clips, soundtracks, and contests. There were fans dressed as Klingons, Vulcans, Federation, and even rare Andorians. Everything I ever wanted to know about Star Trek was there. In the main session actress Marina Sirtis (Counselor Deanna Troi on *Star Trek: The Next Generation*) was the keynote attraction. When she walked in the room people exploded in applause. One fan ran forward with flowers and gave them to her. They hung on every word, laughed at her stories, and lined up for autographs. She was a celebrity.

A decade or so later I attended a very popular Christian convention. I was excited to go and learn new ways of doing ministry. It was everything you wanted to know about _____ (fill in whatever you want - worship, leadership, church planting, etc...). There were booths for products, books, and new programs. There were rooms for presentations and workshops. There was social space for fellowship. There were video clips, interviews, and contests. When the keynote speaker came for the main session, the people exploded in applause. They hung on every word, laughed at his stories, and winced at his challenges. They didn't line up for autographs afterward, but I could not deny he was a celebrity.

I have come to believe that the prevalent American Christian culture breeds insecurity in pastors. Some very good things have been tarnished and twisted by our enemy. We minister in an atmosphere that may actually be toxic to our spiritual lungs. Because we've grown up in it, we are not aware how dangerous it is. It is what we know. It is what we are used to It is what we see. It is what we applaud. But it is also suffocating us. I call them the three deadly C's - Celebritism, Consumerism, and Competition. Even though there's a connection between them, let's look at each separately.

Celebritism

For 11 years the syndicated TV show *Lifestyles of the Rich & Famous* fed viewers images of the extravagant lifestyles of entertainers, athletes and corporate leaders. These kingpins became the envy of young people. Who wouldn't want to be a celebrity? Success, fame, and fortune were marks of fulfilling the American dream. The hit show *American Idol* offered the same picture and promised that anyone had a chance to be famous. Without knowing it, might we have equated success with fame?

> **We minister in an atmosphere that may actually be toxic to our spiritual lungs.**

The American church is highlighted by celebrities. Not that it's their fault, but mega-church pastors, movement leaders, worship leaders, and popular authors have risen to celebrity status among Christians. They faithfully served God and then were blessed with large churches, transformative ministries, or best-selling books. The problem was not their "success," but that it happened in a culture where fame is so highly valued. An entire generation was primed for celebritism and it naturally and subversively carried over into the Church.

You have to wonder if something similar was going on in Corinth when Paul wrote, "What I mean is that each one of you says, 'I follow Paul,' or 'I follow Apollos,' or 'I follow Cephas,' or 'I follow Christ.' Is Christ divided? Was Paul crucified for you? Or were you baptized in the name of Paul?" (1 Corinthians 1:12-13 ESV)

When Francis Chan stepped to the platform at an *Exponential Conference* in Orlando, the 4000+ in attendance roared in approval. He quickly waved them down and then to everyone's surprise, boldly criticized this "celebrity status" he had achieved. In one interview he explained it this way, "I'm glad that there is so much solid teaching available. However, I am struggling with the celebrity status that comes from this kind of exposure. It's not healthy for the preacher, nor is it healthy for those who talk about their ministry heroes so often (I am guilty of this). In many ways, we are conforming to the pattern of the world."[1] Similarly I hear Christians in our churches talk about speakers, authors, and musicians in the same way that people today react to entertainers and athletes.

This mentality is cruel to pastors for multiple reasons. First, people in our churches compare us to these celebrities. Do we speak as well as they do? Are we as funny? As relevant? Do we exposit as well? They compare our churches with their ministries. How come our worship isn't as dynamic? Why don't we have a program for divorced single unemployed moms with children under 3 who don't have cars? The proliferation of celebritism has bred congregants who expect pastors to match up with the "stars of the faith." It will be very difficult for even the strongest pastor to not feel insecure.

Secondly, celebritism sets a standard for success. It's all about size and numbers. How many followers do you have? How many in Sunday attendance? A big ministry means that you're a success. Small is, well, not so good. We celebrate the "wins" of large numbers. We share the stories of church plants that have 100s at their launch service. We invite the "successful" pastors (i.e., pastors of large churches) to speak at our conferences. Therefore, many pastors compete within themselves to prove themselves. If they didn't struggle with whispers from their past, they now have to deal with loud voices in the present. It doesn't take long to feel insecure.

One young pastor shared with me that he was seduced into thinking that success was measured by speaking tours and mega churches. He had pursued it, traveled all over the world, pastored a large church, but ended up losing his wife to another man. Today he admits that all that success was actually failure.

I recall starting my church with a vision of becoming the new powerhouse church in the region. There was a big church in the county north of us and another in the county south, but none in our county. My church was going to be that church. Honestly I wasn't looking for fame or to be a celebrity; I actually had a personal value of developing leaders. Nonetheless, I was raised in a church growth mentality where that was how you graded success so that's what I was going to do. As a result, when my church did not grow like I wanted, I felt like a failure.

Celebritism breeds insecurity.

Consumerism

Americans are consumers.
Buy it.
Use it.
Discard it.

Our economy runs on it. Companies depend on it. Product placement is now common place in movies. Sports arenas and stadiums are now named after companies. From birth to death we are constantly bombarded with messages to get us to want something. I laugh when I hear sports plays being sponsored by products and companies. "That double play was a Jiffy Lube double play!" Good or bad, whether we are aware of it or not, it shapes how we live.

Nancy came into our small group meeting that night all excited. She had spent the day shopping. She shared with some of the other women all the sales she found. I remember hearing her say, "We really didn't need it, but it was such a great deal." Nancy and her husband did quite well financially so it wasn't an issue, but my wife and I were struggling as new church planters. It was such a waste to me that she buy something she didn't need. But that is how our culture is. Want it. Buy it.

We see this craze played out in the endless smart phone race. We may not need the new upgrade, but it's the newer cooler version. See something better. Toss the other, buy the new. Consumerism is "the protection or promotion of the interests of consumers." (Merriam-Webster's) Therefore, it is all about me, my wants, my pleasures, my comforts. Maybe the Apostle John would call it the "lust of the eyes" (1 John 2:16) and warn us, "Little children, keep yourselves from idols." (1 John 5:21) The Apostle Paul might dismiss consumerism for the believer when he writes, "He died for all, that those who live might no longer live for themselves but for him who for their sake died and was raised. (2 Corinthians 5:15)

The Insecure Pastor

In my 30 years as a pastor I have observed that most people treat churches like they do stores, restaurants, and companies. They choose to shop at a particular store based on what the store offers them. Does it have what they're looking for? Does it offer a good deal? Will it provide good customer service? In the same way, many people go church shopping asking the same type of questions. Moreover, many churches are designed to appeal to our consumerism. They advertise, promote, and set up programs that appeal to the felt needs of people. My new church had an advertising slogan, "A Sound Investment for the Entire Family." I felt it was far more attractive than, "Come, die to self with us!" This behavior makes logical sense when you realize that all of us have been raised in consumerism - it's our natural way of thinking!

__Just because it's logical and natural, doesn't necessarily mean it's good for us__.

Just because it's logical and natural, however, doesn't necessarily mean it's good for us. Consumerism breeds insecurity in pastors. Since we are trying to attract people we put a tremendous amount of energy into our promotional image as leaders and as churches. In reality we are trying to win and keep customers. Or maybe we are trying to make and keep them happy?

Every person who left my church ripped my heart out. It didn't matter what the reason, I'd grieve. I'd doubt myself. I'd wonder what I did wrong or why I wasn't good enough. One time I compiled all the reasons people left and told my leadership team that the only common denominator was me so maybe I should leave. They disagreed, but it was still obvious from my thinking that something must be wrong with me -- insecurity was a dominant force in my mind.

Consumerism puts us at the whim of people. Their interests. Their desires. Their needs. We are only as good as our last sermon or the last program that met their needs. Our blood pressure rises with every text from so and so. We flinch when the phone rings. Acid flows up our esophagus when she grabs us after service, "Pastor, can we talk?" It's no wonder we are warned, "The fear of man lays a snare, but whoever trusts in the Lord is safe." (Proverbs 29:25 ESV)

Consumerism feeds that fear and births insecurity.

Competition

My two boys loved to play baseball. We spent many days at the local fields watching them play and interacting with neighbors and townsfolk. There were years when I coached teams, as well. I still drive by the fields in the summer and long for those days. They were fun and enjoyable times, but they were also vicious! Parents yelling at umpires, complaining to coaches, and pushing their kids to win. In the early ages of T-ball we didn't keep score; we wanted the kids to learn the game. But I noticed some little boys keeping score and I overheard some parents doing the same. It was all about winning to them.

Youth sports has become big business. It goes along with most everything in our culture. My daughter was a musician and there was great pressure to compete there, too. If the kids aren't competing for awards and scholarships, then parents are competing for them, somehow living their own lives through their kids. Throw in fantasy sports, gambling, workplace competition for promotions, Christmas decorating competitions, etc....

Compare.

Put down.

Win.

When I was starting my church in 1991 we used a telemarketing program to contact prospective church members. Though we made sure to screen out regular church attendees, I still received a call from a local pastor complaining that we were trying to steal people. I tried to explain how we were specifically looking for those who did not attend a local church. He did not believe me. Instead during the entire conversation I felt like he was my opponent and that we were competing.

I saw this again when I began looking into church planting in Philadelphia. I was told in no uncertain terms that churches in "the city of brotherly love" do not work together! Instead they compete and fight over turf and people. It's not much better in the suburbs. When the big mega-church comes to your area and snatches up people from your church, suddenly you feel like you are in competition. I remember a little church popping up in my town in a small building a few years back. My first reaction was, "What do they think they're doing in MY town?" The competitive juices leak out. The truth is that competition divides.

When Paul wrote against the pseudo-celebritism in Corinth it was in the context of unity. "I appeal to you, brothers, by the name of our Lord Jesus Christ, that all of you agree, and that there be no divisions among you, but that you be united in the same mind and the same judgment. For it has been reported to me by Chloe's people that there is quarreling among you, my brothers. What I mean is that each one of you says, "I follow Paul," or "I follow Apollos," or "I follow Cephas," or "I follow Christ." Is Christ divided? Was Paul crucified for you? Or were you baptized in the name of Paul?" (1 Corinthians 1:10-14 ESV) There was no reason to compete because we are united in Christ.

Jesus ran into the attitude of competition among the disciples. On one occasion James and John had their mom go to Jesus to leverage special treatment for them. When the rest of the disciples heard about it they were angry. Jesus put competition into perspective, "Whoever would be great among you must be your servant, and whoever would be first among you must be your slave, even as the Son of Man came not to be served but to serve, and to give his life as a ransom for many." (Matthew 20:25-28) Two more times (Luke 9 & 22) the disciples argued and competed for top ranking. Both times Jesus the flipped competitive spirit inside out by pointing out that God's perspective on winning is way different than ours..

Jesus even prayed for our generation, "I do not ask for these only, but also for those who will believe in me through their word, that they may all be one, just as you, Father, are in me, and I in you, that they also may be in us, so that the world may believe that you have sent me. The glory that you have given me I have given to them, that they may be one even as we are one, I in them and you in me, that they may become perfectly one, so that the world may know that you sent me and loved them even as you loved me." (John 17:20-23 ESV)

Left unchecked competition grows alongside the other two Deadly C's and fosters insecurity in us. We start comparing ministries, attendance, budgets. Those comparisons grow inside us swelling pride and bringing doubt. We become protective and hoard people, money, ideas. We want our church to get the credit. We are suspicious of other pastors and churches. We don't trust the intentions of others.

Meanwhile our congregants also see other churches as rival companies fighting for the same slice of the Christian consumer pie. They may even pick up on our attitude and exaggerate it to an 'us vs. them' mentality. Like Batman versus Superman or Iron Man versus Captain America we may be two heroes fighting for justice but we do it differently. All the while we feel and know that our way is most assuredly the right way.

The Church is divided. Its power is dissipated. The world sees it as fractured and unloving. Moreover there is no safe place for pastors. There is no security in conferences, ministerium, or fellowships. A pastor cannot be vulnerable with his church because people might leave and then he'd lose to the church down the road. And if we wire-tapped his heart, we'd hear: "I can trust no one. I am alone. I am on my own. I am an insecure pastor."

FOR YOUR OWN REFLECTION:

1. Where do you see consumerism in your own life?

2. Where do you see celebritism in your own dreams?

3. Where do you see competition in your heart?

4. How have any of these shaped how you do ministry?

5. Where do these seep out in your life or ministry?

---

[1] - www.churchleaders.com *3 Questions with Francis Chan*

6

Moses: Finding Strength in Your Inadequacy

My Life Verse: Such confidence we have through Christ toward God. Not that we are adequate in ourselves to consider anything as coming from ourselves, but our adequacy is from God." - 2 Corinthians 3:4-5 NASB

"I will never plant a church." Yes, that is what I said in 1989. I had made an objective assessment of my gifts, strengths, and weaknesses and concluded that I could not do it. Little did I know I would plant Hope Chapel just two years later.

Ten years ago my District Superintendent took me aside to tell me he was resigning and that he wanted to suggest me as one of those to be considered for the role. I had no aspirations to be a District Superintendent. I did not know anyone in the denomination outside my own little circle. I did not think I was qualified. I was quite comfortable leading my church. A few years later I left my church to serve alongside our new District Superintendent.

Planting a church. Leading a group of churches. Writing a book. Honestly I hesitated for each because I am insecure. I am inadequate. I am afraid of failing, of being rejected, of the uncertainty each new challenge brings. But I have learned I don't need to know how to do something if I know God is calling me to do it.

I see a similar theme carried out in the life of Moses. It is a story we are all familiar with, but I want to examine it through the lens of insecurity.

Generations after Joseph brings his family to Egypt, the Israelites have become a threat to the Egyptians. Their numbers have risen rapidly despite slavery and mistreatment. Pharaoh finally gives the order to have every newborn son killed by drowning them in the

Nile River. One family hides their baby son, Moses, in a basket and floats him down the Nile in hopes of saving his life. Pharaoh's daughter discovers this baby and basically adopts him into the royal family.

In the royal family Moses knows he is different. Amazingly he is still raised by his Jewish mother so he knows the truth of his heritage. Moses' early life is in the spotlight since members of Pharaoh's family are celebrities in that society; the Pharaoh himself was worshipped as a god. There is sibling rivalry and competition in the Egyptian family as brothers vie for future leadership positions. As the adopted son Moses may not have been as easily accepted. He is an outsider and deep inside he knows he doesn't belong.

Many years later, after Moses had grown up, he watches an Egyptian beat one of the Jews. After checking to see if he's being watched, he kills the Egyptian and buries him to cover up his action. The Pharaoh hears about it though and seeks to kill Moses. Having failed to help his people, Moses runs away. He starts a new life away from the privileges and comforts of the royal family. He becomes a shepherd and starts a family. Life is so different and so much safer.

Years pass Moses is tending sheep when he notices a bush on fire but not burning up. He goes to check it out and ends up having a dialogue with God.

The Lord said, "So now, go. I am sending you to Pharaoh to bring my people the Israelites out of Egypt."

But Moses said to God, "Who am I that I should go to Pharaoh and bring the Israelites out of Egypt?"

And God said, "I will be with you. And this will be the sign to you that it is I who have sent you: When you have brought the people out of Egypt, you will worship God on this mountain."

Moses said to God, "Suppose I go to the Israelites and say to them, 'The God of your fathers has sent me to you,' and they ask me, 'What is his name?' Then what shall I tell them?"

God said to Moses, "I AM WHO I AM. This is what you are to say to the Israelites: 'I am has sent me to you.'" God also said to Moses, "Say to the Israelites, 'The Lord, the God of your fathers—the God of Abraham, the God of Isaac and the God of Jacob—has sent me to you.'" God also told him all how He was going to deliver his people from the Egyptians and fulfill His promises..

Moses answered, "What if they do not believe me or listen to me and say, 'The Lord did not appear to you'?"

Then the Lord said to him, "What is that in your hand?"

"A staff," he replied.

The Lord said, "Throw it on the ground." Moses threw it on the ground and it became a snake, and he ran from it. Then the Lord said to him, "Reach out your hand and take it by the tail." So Moses reached out and took hold of the snake and it turned back into a staff in his hand. "This," said the Lord, "is so that they may believe that the Lord, the God of their fathers—the God of Abraham, the God of Isaac and the God of Jacob—has appeared to you." The Lord also gave him two more signs to use: his hand turning leprous and turning water into blood.

Moses said to the Lord, "Pardon your servant, Lord. I have never been eloquent, neither in the past nor since you have spoken to your servant. I am slow of speech and tongue."

The Lord said to him, "Who gave human beings their mouths? Who makes them deaf or mute? Who gives them sight or makes them blind? Is it not I, the Lord? Now go; I will help you speak and will teach you what to say."

But Moses said, "Pardon your servant, Lord. Please send someone else."

Then the Lord's anger burned against Moses and he said, "What about your brother, Aaron the Levite? I know he can speak well. He is already on his way to meet you, and he will be glad to see you. You shall speak to him and put words in his mouth; I will help both of you speak and will teach you what to do. He will speak to the people for you, and it will be as if he were your mouth and as if you were God to him. But take this staff in your hand so you can perform the signs with it."

(Excerpted from Exodus 3-4 NIV)

I see significant points in this story that can relate to our insecurity. In particular there are insights in Moses' objections and God's responses to him. We know that Moses is coming out of a time of life that may very well have left him insecure, unsure of himself, and unwilling to risk anymore. He's lived in the fishbowl of a royal family, lived amongst the competition of rival brothers, and lived as an outsider in secret. He failed miserably in helping his people when he tried it on his own before. He's on the run and now settled down in a new life.

Two things show up to me in Moses' objections. First, he sees only his own inabilities. He knows himself really well. He knows he cannot rescue his people. He tried before and look where it got him. Look at what he says:

> Who am **I**?
> What do **I** tell them?
> What if they don't believe **me**?
> **I** am slow of speech....

Moses is focused only on himself. He can only comprehend what he himself can do. I bet that if he answers the question of "who am I?" he thinks, "I am weak. I am a reject. I am a failure." It comes up in all of his responses to God in this dialogue. He brings up one reason after another why he cannot do what God says.

At the crux of insecurity is the question of belief.

When I was sent to plant my church the Church Planting Director questioned my pastor, "Who is this guy? He can't plant a church." My District Superintendent encouraged me, "We know this is difficult so we don't expect anything. If it doesn't work, we won't hold it against you." There were those in our church who doubted the wisdom, "Why would you want to start a church in THAT neighborhood?" One believer who lived in the town warned me, "God can't do anything in Pine Hill." I may not have known how to plant a new church, but what I did know was that I needed to do what God was telling me to do.

Second observation about Moses is that he doesn't know what God is like firsthand. He knows his own inabilities, but he doesn't know God's abilities. His heritage and faith stories were passed on orally through his mother. He had heard about Abraham, Isaac, Jacob, and Joseph, but he had yet to see God work. For hundreds of years his people lived in slavery and misery. Is God really great? Is God really good? Is God really glorious? Is He really gracious? Moses is facing his very own unbelief before the burning bush.

The Insecure Pastor

At the crux of our insecurity is the question of belief. Who am I going to believe? My own experience or God's word? Will my own failures in the past determine who God is now and in the future? Insecurity is always about two contrasting truths - my inabilities and God's abilities. Which one will I lean on?

Curt Schilling, former major league pitcher for the Phillies, Diamondbacks, and Red Sox, was about to start game 6 of the 2004 ALCS. The Red Sox were attempting to do what was never done before and rally from a 3-0 game deficit to beat their arch rivals, the Yankees. Curt had pitched and lost the first game of the series. He was intent on pitching again despite an ankle injury. He had undergone a surgical procedure the day before to stabilize a tendon. By the time the game was done, his white sock was soaked in blood. By the time the series was done, history was made and then Boston went on to win its first world championship since 1918.

There is story behind the headlines though. I met Curt years before around the time he became a Christian. Over the years we corresponded regularly with prayer requests, Bible studies, discussions, and Q&A as I encouraged him in his new faith. It was no surprise when I got a phone call the afternoon of that Game 6. He wanted me to pray for him pitching that night. I will never forget the conversation.

"Curt, you know I am a Yankees fan."

"I know. I don't want you to pray for me to win. It's just that in game one it was all me out on the mound. I want to do it tonight in God's strength, not mine. Win or lose."

I paused for a brief second before saying, "Okay, I can pray for that." When I prayed with him over the phone I went one step further and asked that "he would experience Your presence on the mound like never before."

After the game the FOX announcer asked Curt how his ankle was feeling. Curt surprisingly responded, "Before that, let me say I became a Christian 7 years ago and tonight I experienced God's presence out there like never before." For the first time Curt was publically acknowledging his faith. The next day he called me and admitted that he had nothing on the mound. He was exhausted. He ached. He didn't have command, control, or pop. He specifically said that he threw balls down the heart of the plate and the Yankees missed them. It would make no sense to anyone except the two of us. We knew that his inabilities were overshadowed by God's immense abilities ... even in a game of baseball.

I found how God response to Moses parallels the ways he has dealt with my own insecurity. Over the years he has met my own insecurity head on with remarkably similar expressions of truth.

His first response is simply, "I will be with you." Our insecurity is counteracted by the reality of God's PRESENCE. When he is near, our courage rises. When we are convinced we are not alone and it doesn't depend all on us, then we can move forward in confidence. I saw this visually in the *Prince Caspian* movie when little Lucy with her small knife stands on a bridge to block and stop a large army of well armed soldiers. It looks foolish and impossible until the camera pans back and we see the mighty lion Aslan standing behind her. His presence gave her courage.

We experience God's presence in a variety of ways. In the classic *Practicing the Presence of God* Brother Lawrence shares his journey of bringing God into every aspect of daily life. From an inner strength of faith to a supernatural manifestation of power, God demonstrates his active presence in our lives. In the first year of my church plant I made it a pattern of going for a walk in the woods on Monday mornings. God always seemed to meet me there. Most of the time it was quiet reminders of His word, but on a couple occasions when I was going through some very dark times it was supernatural and beyond explanation.

In recent years I have made an effort to not just try to bring God into my daily activities, but also to separate myself and to focus on his presence. New habits of midday meditation, solitude & silence, and spontaneous worship have relaxed me and freed me from a lot of worry and anxiety. My insecurity melts when I am in his presence.

God's next response to Moses is "I AM WHO I AM." Our insecurity is overshadowed by the magnitude of God's PERSON. Remember that Moses did not know what God is really like so God tells him. God is simply I AM. He is completely self-sufficient and is not dependent on any person or thing. He is utterly above and beyond all of creation. The name Yahweh appears to be related in Hebrew to this phrase I AM. This means he is unlimited in power, knowledge, presence, wisdom, insight, and any and all abilities. He could play a virtuoso concert for himself. He could construct the most magnificent monument to himself. He could orate the perfect sermon in any language.

The implications of this are staggering. He does not need us. He does not depend on us to get his ministry done. God was going to deliver the Israelites whether Moses was a part of it or not. That means my failures don't mess up his plans. I don't need to be insecure because He doesn't depend on me.

A couple years ago I was asked to speak at one of our Spanish churches. Not only is it difficult to speak with a translator but it was a small church that I don't know too well. I didn't really want to do it, but I reluctantly I agreed. In the week leading up to that Sunday I simply pulled out an old sermon. I did not prepare or review it. I am embarrassed to admit I didn't even pray much about it. That Sunday, as the worship music began, I pretended to sing along in Spanish. About halfway through the music, however, I sensed something very powerful - God was present. I thought to myself, "Oh crap, God is here and I am not ready!" I took a deep breath before preaching wondering if lightning would strike me down. Instead, I felt empowered beyond myself. At one point the translator had tears in his eyes. Some listeners started to cry. After the message the pastor asked me to pray for people as they came forward. I couldn't speak their language and I didn't know their issues, but suddenly I knew what to pray over each person; God was uniquely ministering to each of them. Afterward I knelt in the pew and wept. I was deeply humbled that God used me despite me.

God also responds to Moses, "Now go; I will help you speak and will teach you what to say." We have little reason to be insecure when it's about God's POWER not our own. Speaking about his ministry Paul wrote, "Him we proclaim, warning everyone and teaching everyone with all wisdom, that we may present everyone mature in Christ. For this I toil, struggling with all his energy that he powerfully works within me." (Colossians 1:28-29 ESV) Paul worked hard and put all he had into his ministry, but it was not according to his strength and abilities. So much of pastoral ministry can be done by good people trained in some helpful skills. God is not asking good people to do their best. He is asking broken people to let HIS life and power work through them.

Moses was broken. He may very well have been a shell of a man emotionally. Think about it. He was adopted into a tyrant's household, sat by powerlessly while his family was abused, murdered someone, and then was hunted by the most powerful man in the world at the time. This is not a pilot for a new HBO series, this was Moses' life. God wants to use this broken man, this jar of clay, this common vessel.

God helps Moses with his inability by bringing Aaron alongside him. Moses won't be alone. Our insecurity can be diminished by God's PEOPLE. I started out in ministry wanted to be on my own, separate from any denomination. I guess I wanted to do it my way. That quickly changed after a couple of years. Now I love doing ministry with others. Recently I sat with a young pastor and helped him think through his sermon calendar. He thanked me profusely because, as he put it, you "feel so alone in ministry."

Whether it's because of the 3 Deadly C's or because of pride many pastors suffer from LLS - Lone Leader Syndrome. Not only will they lead without outside support but they won't even trust their own church leaders to do things. At first glance we may think that they don't suffer from insecurity, but I think they do. In many cases they are so afraid of failure that they have to make sure they're in control of everything. They compensate for their insecurity by living in an illusion of control. Sadly pastors who want to be on their own rarely turn out well in the long run.

We need each other. Hebrews 3:13 calls us to, "encourage one another daily, as long as it is called "Today," so that none of you may be hardened by sin's deceitfulness." The overall context is unbelief, the sin and struggle of unbelief. We need each other to see that. We need each other to avoid being sucked under by the rip current of insecurity. Moses only saw himself so God brought Aaron and later the elders of Israel to share in God's ministry. God's strength is available when we are inadequate. God's strength may sometimes actually be God's people. As pastors, we can help each other to focus not on our own inabilities but to focus on God's presence, God's power, and God's person.

FOR YOUR OWN REFLECTION:

1. What are you good at?

2. What are not good at?

3. What is God good at? How is He better than you in what you are good at?

4. How do you tend to stick to those things you are competent at?

5. One author recently declared that we are all "control freaks." If so, then how does that show up in your life, ministry, or family?

7

Joshua: Finding Courage in Your Uncertainty

The Pine Hill Alliance Church board gathered one last time before closing down. The District Superintendent introduced me. I outlined a plan to close the church, re-tool, and re-train whoever wanted to stay, and re-start 10 months later as a brand new church. They asked me if I'd done this before. I admitted I hadn't but was confident God would lead. I was actually thinking, "No, I am only 28 and have never pastored a church, period, much less done something as crazy as this. I have absolutely no idea what will happen nor how to get there!" I was truly entering a land of uncertainty, but I kept my doubts to myself. The week before the new church launched I had a vivid nightmare that no one showed up, except those from the old church -- and they laughed and mocked me!

    18 years later I was starting my new role of Church Planting Director for the Metropolitan District C&MA. I was stepping into the shoes of two great leaders who had done a great job inspiring church planting. How was I going to follow them? What was more complicated was one was now the C&MA Vice President and the other was now my boss. Worse yet I had internalized the grief of my transition and now it was bursting out in anxiety and depression. Where do I start? What do I do? How can I do any better than these guys? What if I don't live up to expectations? I was feeling insecurity at a deeper level than ever before. During that time God used Joshua's story to show me more insights into dealing with insecurity.

    Joshua was a tough guy. Israel obviously did not have an army while in Egypt, but once they were out on their own, Joshua arose as a military leader. In Exodus 17 he led the makeshift army in its first battle. When Moses and he returned from their mountain retreat with God, Joshua assumed the ruckus in camp was the sound of war (Exodus 32:17). When two irresponsible elders started prophesying in the camp, Joshua was competitive and jealous for Moses' leadership and wanted to shut them up (Numbers 11:16-30). He and Caleb were the only spies who wanted to fight for the promised land. When the Lord appeared to him in Joshua 5, it wasn't in a burning bush, but by a warrior with a drawn sword. That's Joshua's language. He's a competitor, a warrior, a tough guy, but he also faces uncertainty and insecurity.

Consider what Joshua's life was before he was put in charge. For at least 40 years he was under Moses' leadership as his assistant and protégé. He enjoyed the safety net and the covering of Moses' leadership. In Exodus 17 during the battle with the Amalekites Joshua leads the soldiers on the battlefield but it is Moses' prayers that carry the day. Joshua was secure knowing Moses was overseeing and praying.

Joshua also enjoyed meeting God with Moses. He went up with Moses to the mountain in Exodus 24. There they experienced together the glory of God and received instruction for worship and life. In Exodus 33 Moses set up a tent for meeting with God. There the Lord would speak face to face with Moses while Joshua was there. We even read in Exodus 33:11 that Joshua would stay in the tent when Moses left. Maybe he wanted to linger in God's presence or maybe he was afraid to go before the people; we are not told. Regardless Joshua's relationship with God was contingent upon Moses.

Joshua also enjoyed not being ultimately responsible. He was in the second chair, the buck did not stop with him; the fate of the nation fell on Moses' decisions not his. There is a huge difference between being the Captain of the ship and being the First Mate or Officer. The ultimate responsibility for the welfare of the ship falls on the Captain. As second in command you follow orders, you give input, but the final decision is the Captain's. Joshua had the emotional freedom of being #2.

It took a month for me to decide to take the opportunity to start a church in Pine Hill. It was not an easy choice. I would have to quit my teaching job and leave a growing healthy church where I admired the Senior Pastor as my mentor. God used an episode of *Star Trek: The Next Generation* to speak to me. The ship's second in command, Commander Riker, was hesitating in taking his own command. Another officer challenged him, "All you know how to do is play it safe. I suppose that's why someone like you sits in the shadow of a great man for as long as you have, passing up one command after another." Later that week as I sat in the church office balking at even considering leaving this successful church, the Spirit reminded me of that quote. I wondered that night, "Am I afraid to take the Captain's chair?"

Joshua had to face a similar situation. He is going to be thrust into the Captain's chair. Moses tells Joshua that he will be his successor and lead the nation. He is then commissioned as the leader (Deuteronomy 31). As I reflect on how Joshua might be feeling I am struck by the last words of Deuteronomy, "And there has not arisen a prophet since in Israel like Moses, whom the LORD knew face to face, none like him for all the signs and the wonders that the LORD sent him to do in the land of Egypt, to Pharaoh and to all his servants and to all his land, and for all the mighty power and all the great deeds of terror that Moses did in the sight of all Israel." (Deuteronomy 34:10-12) That is who Joshua is replacing!

Joshua's insecurity is compounded by the temptation to compare himself to the previous leader. How can I live up to that? Mmm, how did he do that again, so I can duplicate it? What would Moses do? If Moses got in trouble with God, what does that mean for me? Will the people follow me as they did Moses? Will I be as good a leader as Moses was? The questions probably swirled around in Joshua's heart, maybe consciously, but certainly sub-consciously.

The Lord knows exactly what this warrior needs. He knows Joshua so He calls to his inner toughness, to his warrior spirit. Joshua 1 shows us how God speaks to Joshua's insecurity.

First, he reminds him of God's promise. "Every place that the sole of your foot will tread upon I have given to you, *just as I promised to Moses*." (Joshua 1:3 ESV) Notice how God equalizes the comparisons. Moses = Joshua. What I promised Moses, I promise Joshua. No difference. It isn't about either of you, it's about Me. No reason to compare.

Second, he reminds him of God's power and presence. "No man shall be able to stand before you all the days of your life. Just as I was with Moses, so I will be with you. I will not leave you or forsake you." (Joshua 1:3 ESV) We explored this in the previous chapter. Moses starting out in a brand new ministry needed to be reminded of God's power and presence. Joshua continuing that ministry also needs the same truth.

Third, he calls out to who he is. "Be strong and courageous..." which he repeats over and over throughout the chapter and "for you shall cause this people to inherit the land that I swore to their fathers to give them. (Joshua 1:5). It's like God is saying, "be courageous because you are their leader. You will lead them. It will happen." Joshua knows what is needed to be a good warrior. If you are going to win, accomplish the mission, or save lives, you cannot just cut and run. You have to be strong and courageous. You have too risk your own safety, comfort, and life.

Staff Sergeants Ty Carter and Clint Romesha received the nation's highest award for valor, the Medal of Honor for Heroism, for their actions at the Battle of Kamdesh, Afghanistan, on October 3, 2009. This was the first time in fifty five years that two Americans have lived to receive this honor in the same battle.

That night over 300 Taliban insurgents assaulted the American Combat Outpost Keating. The outpost was manned by 53 Americans, an Afghan National Army unit (which quickly broke and ran away during the attack) and its two Latvian trainers. The enemy attack was overwhelming with a barrage of fire from rocket-propelled grenades, anti-aircraft machine guns, heavy machine guns, mortars, snipers and small arms fire.

Early on in the fight, Staff Sergeant Carter ran through heavy fire from one position to another to deliver ammunition. When a fellow soldier was hit, Carter, disregarded his own safety and, figuring that he'd probably die, dashed through enemy fire to rescue the wounded soldier. Meanwhile Staff Sergeant Romesha continually exposed himself to heavy enemy fire. He was continually at the place where the fighting was the heaviest. He led counterattacks to rescue wounded Americans and maintained radio communications with higher commands. The citation reads, "Staff Sgt. Romesha's heroic actions throughout the day-long battle were critical in suppressing an enemy that had far greater numbers."[1]

That is the language Joshua understood. He could not be worried IF he could do it, he had to do it. There was no room for comparing and doubting. Insecurity could not rule. God called out the warrior within him. "Be strong and courageous. This is what I, the Lord of heaven and earth, have called you to do. You will lead."

"Only be strong and very courageous, being careful to do according to all the law that Moses my servant commanded you. Do not turn from it to the right hand or to the left, that you may have good success wherever you go. This Book of the Law shall not depart from your mouth, but you shall meditate on it day and night, so that you may be careful to do according to all that is written in it. For then you will make your way prosperous, and then you will have good success. Have I not commanded you? Be strong and courageous. Do not be frightened, and do not be dismayed, for the Lord your God is with you wherever you go." (Joshua 1:9-9 ESV)

This courage, this heroism that God is commanding is not something that can be generated simply by grunting and getting psyched up. It's not a football game that lasts for a few hours. It is needed 24-7. There needs to be spiritual stamina and endurance. So God elaborates by linking success to knowing, following, talking about, and thinking about God's truth. Clarity for Joshua would come from reviewing over and over everything God told Moses. Confidence would come as he embraced the promises and practices of this new way of living God had laid out for His people. Success would come as he led the people out of his own interaction with God.

Insecurity can be traced to lies, half-truths, and ignorance. I might believe that for life to work out I have to be in control. I might believe that for God to work I have to perform for him. I might not fully understand the depth of his love and acceptance of me. When it comes down to it, I am not believing correctly so I feel insecure, uncertain, unloved, a failure.

When I was in my time of anxiety and depression, I found daily strength and hope by falling back onto what I had learned. I reviewed all the truth I had learned and taught over the years. I went back to memorizing Scripture and meditating throughout the day. I experienced firsthand, "If your law had not been my delight, I would have perished in my affliction." (Psalm 119:92 ESV) I would not have made it through that time without relying upon God's Word to expose my faulty thinking and show me truth.

When I had a staff member who was undermining my leadership and speaking badly of me to church members, it was truth that kept me from responding in defensiveness and anger. Insecurity called me to fight back, to save my honor, to correct the lies, to manage and control the situation. However, I spent a long time that month looking into God's Word. God reminded me of Jesus before his accusers. He showed me David letting God be in control when Absalom rose up to challenge his leadership. The truth deflated insecurity as I accepted that my leadership comes from the Lord. I had to be strong and courageous trusting God to vindicate me, to establish my leadership, and to guide me going forward. And he did.

Joshua would not have made it as a leader without reviewing the words of God passed on through Moses. He needed to know, follow, talk about, and think about truth. The whispers of the past, the doubts of the present, the whims of fickle people, the comparisons to Moses would all conspire to undermine his strength and courage. Truth was his way out of insecurity and into confidence.

FOR YOUR OWN REFLECTION:

1. How do you respond to uncertainty?

2. Where do you get courage from?

3. Who do you compare yourself to?

4. What place does God's Word have in your daily life?

5. Where do you need God's truth to strengthen you today?

---

[1] - https://www.army.mil/medalofhonor/romesha/citation.html

8

David: Finding Security in Being A Nobody

We all know David. He was the famous shepherd boy, the great king, the psalmist, and the slayer of Goliath. He is famous to us. If he were here today, we would hail him as a great pastor and worship leader. Christians would flock to his conferences and concerts. We'd buy his books and listen to his podcasts. He would be a celebrity. But not in his own eyes would he be. As far as David was concerned he was a nobody. He did not see himself as we see him today nor as those in his day saw him.

When King Saul sacrificed his anointing for expediency and selfish gain (1 Samuel 15), God sent the prophet Samuel to the house of Jesse to select a replacement king. When Samuel was wowed by the physical prowess of some of Jesse's sons, the Lord warned him, "Do not look on his appearance or on the height of his stature, because I have rejected him. For the LORD sees not as man sees: man looks on the outward appearance, but the LORD looks on the heart." (1 Samuel 16:7) So Samuel could cross out "biggest baddest looking dude" on the application. God was more interested in a right heart than a chiseled body.

One by one Samuel dismissed Jesse's sons. After the seventh one, Samuel realized that none of those present were chosen by God. Wondering what's up, he asked the dad, "Are all your sons here?" The dad admits that the youngest is missing and is out tending the sheep. Was David not present because he was being responsible for his assigned job? Was he not invited? For that matter why was he relegated to the "lowest role" on the family farm? As you may recall being a shepherd was not a coveted career in that society. To make matters worse, his brothers did not think well of him. In one scene when he shows up on the battlefield and questions about Goliath, his eldest brother gets angry and accuses David. "Why have you come down? And with whom have you left those few sheep in the wilderness? I know your presumption and the evil of your heart, for you have come down to see the battle." (1 Samuel 17:28) He's irritated with his little brother hanging around the army. He accuses him of being a voyeur, of being irresponsible, and of showing up the troops. David's response infers that this is a pattern, "What have I done *now*?" {emphasis mine} David may be wondering if he can ever do anything right for his brother. It sounds like the prototypical younger brother feeling lost in the shadow of older siblings. Based on this interaction I think David was intentionally left out of Samuel's interview process because his family did not think he was good enough.

Despite what his family thought of him, David had a lot going for him. He was good looking with a tan complexion and beautiful eyes (1 Samuel 16:12). He was well spoken, fine looking, brave, a good fighter, and musically talented (1 Samuel 16:18). Moreover, we are told that the Lord was with him. He later goes on to kill Goliath. The entire nation heard about David's exploits. Women sang songs about him. He became a celebrity who would have been interviewed on *Good Morning Israel* right away. He was headline news. Nonetheless, when he is approached to marry the king's daughter his response is telling, "Does it seem to you a little thing to become the king's son-in-law, since I am a poor man and have no reputation?" (1 Samuel 18:23) Another translation has David saying he is "little known." Despite all his popularity, exploits, and success, he still sees himself as a nobody. He feels insecure no matter what others say or think.

> **Ruminating deep within the insecure pastor's heart is the temptation to prove oneself.**

It makes sense for David to feel insecure. The words and attitudes of his family echoed through his heart (aka. whispers from the past). King Saul, his father-in-law and potential father figure, threw spears at him. Then forced him to live as a fugitive on the run. His new wife Michel ended up mocking him and disrespecting him when he worshipped the Lord with abandon (2 Samuel 6). Emotionally and physically, David is insecure. That insecurity was reinforced by his brother, by Saul, and by Michel. It's no wonder that even as king, David saw himself as a nobody.

The temptation to prove himself and validate himself must have been great for David. This might be what fueled his decision to perform a census in disobedience of God (2 Samuel 24 and 1 Chronicles 21). The numbering of able-bodied males for military service would certainly boost a king's perception of strength and security. This would be especially pertinent after the great victories over the Philistines where Goliath's brothers were killed (1 Chronicles 20). Look at my great army and what it accomplished! I am someone.

This may also have been what fueled his adultery with Bathsheba (2 Samuel 11). Instead of leading his army into battle David hangs out at home. In his boredom and lack of striving for success on the battlefield, he seeks another kind of conquest - sexual. David seduced, maybe even coerced, Bathsheba and they had sex. Look at me. I can get whatever I want! I am somebody!

Ruminating deep within the insecure pastor's heart is the temptation to prove oneself. We wrestle with temptations similar to David's. Some strive to prove themselves in the ministry. They work hard to validate what they do, gain a name for themselves and be successful. They sacrifice family, principles, spiritual vitality, and physical health to do so. Many will "cut corners" on leadership qualifications, exaggerate numbers, or even plagiarize sermons. Others shepherd under the critical eye of others' expectations; they strain themselves to please people and gain enough acceptance. There are some who look to other avenues to discover that elusive sense of significance. One pastor I knew became addicted to golf and frizzled away many hours every day on the green. Sports, video games, exercise, online investing, anything that we feel competent in or that gives us a feeling of success, these become idols of our hearts - compensations for our insecurity.

One author puts it this way, "Every one of us has people or possessions we turn to or attitudes or behaviors we fall back on when life does not go the way we want it to. Counterfeit affections exert a strong pull, even when we realize they are counterfeit. Sometimes it is easier to hold onto the familiar, and make it our lifeline even if it does not satisfy, than to risk letting go in order to grab hold of something else that will."[1]

There were a few incidences where David handled insecurity inappropriately, but there are more positive examples. In times when the circumstances of life were most insecure, David seemed most secure. He relied on the person, the presence, the power, and the people of God. We get a glimpse of his heart when we read his prayers and songs in the Psalms. They are raw and honest windows into his soul. He does not hold anything back.

- He does not Christianize his prayers before writing them for all to see - "Let them be blotted out of the book of the living" (Psalm 69:28).
- We hear his doubts - "Why are you so far from saving me, from the words of my groaning?" (Psalm 22:1)
- We feel his anger - "May his children be fatherless and his wife a widow! (Psalm 109:9)
- We dive into his lows - "Why are you cast down, O my soul, and why are you in turmoil within me?" (Psalm 42:5)
- We identify with his anxiety - " I am upset and disturbed. My mind is filled with apprehension and with gloom." (Psalm 6:3)
- We experience the darkness of his depression - "Darkness is my closest friend" (Psalm 88:18).

We ride the rollercoaster of his emotions as he wrestles with God's faithfulness and goodness in an uncertain and insecure life. David's solution to insecurity was an intimacy with God.

I want to highlight three historical events that serve as a backdrop for these prayers and songs. The first is David on the run from King Saul. His life is threatened. He has no safe place to be in Israel. He has to leave home and family. Saul has mobilized the army to hunt him down, but David is not left to himself. He has an inside man - Jonathan, the king's son - who is a great friend and supporter. He has a group of men with him, warriors who want to follow him. He is not alone. It is no wonder that he wrote Psalm 133 - "Behold, how good and pleasant it is when brothers dwell in unity!"

In the midst of my depression I unexpectedly showed up at my church's worship service on Sunday. A good friend and elder looked at me, 'What are you doing here?! I didn't expect to see you here." I replied, "Well, for years I've taught that when we are down we need each other and shouldn't isolate ourselves." Sure enough I remember feeling "at home" that day, feeling safe with "family," and that I was not alone. Granted not every church will provide those positive feelings, but there is a circle of people God has for each one of us to connect with. Pastors and leaders who choose to keep others at a distance suffer because for whatever reason (my hunch is that it's insecurity and fear!) they choose to be alone. I had lunch this week with seven pastors who had just completed a two year learning cohort. One of them shared, "I really appreciated our time together. I know now I can go to any of you with anything." There was plenty of agreement and many words of encouragement. Serving in different churches all over southern New Jersey, these men are not alone. Insecurity is diminished as we believe in each other, treat each other with value, and pour into each other's lives.

The second event is David's establishing of a tabernacle for the Lord in 1 Chronicles 15-16. After David's fame increased he constructed buildings in Jerusalem for himself. He then put up a tent on one of his properties for the ark of the Lord. He was intent on not only honoring God but setting apart a place for the tangible presence of God which the ark was. After the huge initial celebration David set up a daily system of prayer and worship in that tent. Many musicians, singers, Levites, and priests were assigned to worship every day, if not 24/7. David demonstrated to the entire nation that God's presence was vital for their success. Worship would be the engine of the nation. During this time, out of his heart, sprang many of the psalms (prayers and songs) of Israel. It appears David longs for God's presence; that longing is repeated throughout his songs and prayers. He wanted it so much that he re-oriented his property, his nation, his daily rhythm to experience it.

A couple of years ago I was having a hard time believing God is good. My adult children were struggling; there was financial hardship, emotional trouble, conflict, and even suicidal ideation. Churches were not growing; there was conflict and complaints; some pastors were failing and falling. I couldn't reconcile the fact that God was allowing these things to happen to those I loved. There were days I was upset with God to say the least. I knew I was not believing that God is good. I would say He was, but I felt powerless to change my feelings. One morning I was struck by Exodus 33:18-19 - Moses said, "Please show me your glory." And he said, "I will make all my goodness pass before you and will proclaim before you my name 'The

Lord.'" Suddenly I recognized there was a direct connection between God's goodness and God's presence. The only way for me to see God's goodness was not to have trouble cease, brokenness healed, or churches grow, but to experience God's presence. So I began a journey that year to discover anew the reality of God's manifest presence ... and sometime in the last quarter of the year I no longer doubted God's goodness. I can't say exactly when it was because I was more thinking about pursuing His presence. The more I experienced His presence, the less I questioned His goodness.

Theologically I know God is omnipresent, that he is everywhere. Experientially, however, I am not always aware of Him. Most of us know the difference between being present and not 'being present' - we're home with the family, but our minds are churning about the church! I think a better analogy is that which we have experienced with our dog. When we are home, he is more at ease; he knows we are there and he's fine. But when we call him onto our laps, scratch him, snuggle with him, whisper that he is a good boy, he lights up, and his tail wags furiously. In very tangible ways he experiences our presence, our acceptance, and our love. I think this is the difference between knowing God is present and experiencing God's presence. I think this is what David meant when he spoke of God's presence.

My favorite psalm is Psalm 16 which ends with "in your presence there is fullness of joy." Obviously the ultimate experience is when I die, but the first fruits or the taste of heaven are in experiencing His presence here and now. Some call it the manifest presence of God. Basically it's when God shows up - he heals, he does a miracle, his word jumps off the page, he comforts, he speaks prophetically, he convicts, he delivers, he does something supernatural, or he simply arranges a coincidence that has no other explanation but divine. Like David I have found the more I experience God's presence, the less insecure I am. When my daily quiet time or devotion is more than a mundane obligatory task, but an encounter with the living God, I enjoy a sense of confidence not rooted in my own successes or failures.

The third event is when one of David's sons led a coup and rebelled against King David (2 Samuel 13-19). Over a period of four years Absalom undermined the king's credibility. He secretly manipulated people to think of himself as likeable, helpful, wise, and approachable. He subtly made himself look better than David. When he announced his claim for the throne, many supported him. When the coup was in full swing, David fled the city. David's initial response showed more security than insecurity. Rather than rush to defend himself and fight back, he relinquished the throne. It's almost as though the throne is not his source of significance or security. Something greater was. Someone greater was. David's trust in God's greatness is what motivates his response. God is in control so he doesn't have to be. If his reign is over, that's God's to decide.

One pastor I knew responded to a potential coup by a pastoral staff member by holding on tighter to his "throne." His leadership became more controlling, more demanding, more restrictive. He interpreted any disagreement as rebellion. He tolerated no one who offered alternative views. The church was **his**. It took awhile before the elders finally dismissed him because of his abusive leadership. He did not go quietly and fought back verbally and legally. David, on the other hand, held his throne with an open hand. He was secure not in his position, but in his God.

The youth pastor who undermined my leadership in his short time with our church did not respect my leadership and wanted to do his own thing. After his dismissal he continued to badmouth me and promote himself to those in our church. Later he even accused me in an email of being a megalomaniac. People were concerned and called me to defend myself. Because I had been reading David's story, I chose not to speak up, defend myself, or attack him. I would be silent. I would trust God to defend me or, if necessary, to dismiss me. That was a tremendously freeing decision for me especially when I watched God vindicate me and silence him.

David did not choose to be king. He saw himself as a nobody. That didn't, however, cause him to be paralyzed in insecurity. His heart was bent toward the Lord; he was continually pursuing intimacy with God. He enjoyed an experience of the presence of God in worship and prayer that emboldened him to know and trust God. He did not have to be king to be someone. He discovered that he was someone, someone special to the God of the universe.

I'm an open book to you; even from a distance, you know what I'm thinking.
You know when I leave and when I get back; I'm never out of your sight.
You know everything I'm going to say before I start the first sentence.
I look behind me and you're there, then up ahead and you're there, too—
   your reassuring presence, coming and going.
This is too much, too wonderful— I can't take it all in!
Psalm 139:2-6 MSG

FOR YOUR OWN REFLECTION:

1. When you were young, were you an outsider or an insider? How popular or recognized were you?

2. How did God's calling affect you?

Recall the times in your life when you sensed God's presence.

3. How were they different than other times?

4. What did it do for you? ...in you?

5. Were you doing anything different to initiate that experience?

6. What role do you think worship might have in this? ...the Word? ...the community of faith?

---

[1] - Frost, J. (2006). *Spiritual Slavery to Spiritual Sonship*. Shippensburg, PA: Destiny Image

9

Jeremiah: Finding Confidence in Your Inexperience

When I was a kid one of my favorite TV shows was GET SMART. The show followed the exploits of bumbling Secret Agent 86, Maxwell Smart and his female partner Agent 99. Max always portrayed himself as confident, suave, and intelligent, but in reality he was often inexperienced, naive, and dumb. When 99 would present a plan, Max would respond with, "If you don't mind, 99, I'd like to figure this out myself." He then would pause and repeat 99's idea as his plan! Even after all his apologies ("Sorry about that, Chief") and his failures ("That's the second time I fell for that this week!"), the forces of virtue triumphed over the forces of rottenness.

In my initial years of ministry I felt like Maxwell Smart. As a brand new youth pastor, the parents and the pastor asked me what I was going to do so I shared a clear vision and plan of what I was going to do with their kids. It sounded good, but I had no idea what I was doing. I never wanted to be a youth pastor nor did I have any training for dealing with teenagers. Like Max I portrayed the facade that I knew what I was doing, but inside I wondered, "What the heck am I doing?"

I remember a few years into our church plant I asked my key leaders, "So when do we feel like grownups?" We were successfully planting a church. We were breaking down walls and overcoming great odds. We were seeing things happen others only dreamed of. Sure, we had a clear vision and philosophy of ministry, but we really did not know what we were doing. We still felt like kids, young and inexperienced.

We all start off young and inexperienced. For many of us there also is an inner insecurity. For some it's masked by bravado or a facade of confidence. For some it creeps out in relational conflict or a controlling spirit. For others it paralyzes them from doing anything risky or new. And so it was with a young prophet called by God to speak to a region of people in spiritual and national turmoil. Here's the conversation between God and Jeremiah:

> Now the word of the Lord came to me, saying, "Before I formed you in the womb I knew you, and before you were born I consecrated you; I appointed you a prophet to the nations."
>
> Then I said, "Ah, Lord God! Behold, I do not know how to speak, for I am only a youth."
>
> But the Lord said to me, "Do not say, 'I am only a youth'; for to all to whom I send you, you shall go, and whatever I command you, you shall speak. Do not be afraid of them, for I am with you to deliver you, declares the Lord." Then the Lord put out his hand and touched my mouth. And the Lord said to me, "Behold, I have put my words in your mouth. (Jeremiah 1:4-9 ESV)

Jeremiah was being thrust into ministry by the Lord. Though he grew up in a Levitical household he obviously did not feel prepared for what God was calling him to. He was young and inexperienced. Not only had he not done this particular ministry before, but probably had not done any other ministry either; thus he was left with no experience to build from. Moreover, he did not even have the life experience to draw from. Finally, he admitted that his speaking skills were not good. Truly Jeremiah was incompetent, unskilled, and untrained.

For me it is the Lord's response that demonstrates where genuine confidence comes from. Like a superhero, He holds up his finger and says, "I got this. You just stay behind me." Once again His words echo the same truths embraced by Moses, Joshua, and David - His presence, His power, His person, His people.

God designed Jeremiah, fashioned him in the womb, carefully crafted him for the good works, which God prepared beforehand, that *he* should walk in them. If anyone knows Jeremiah, God does. Jeremiah does not even know what he is capable of. I sure didn't. Over and over, God put me in situations that I did not think I could do - the first funeral, the first church discipline, the first time I watched someone die and then had to tell the spouse, the first key family that left our church, the first conflict with a staff member, the first baby who died, the first message to preach without any preparation, the first building project, the first rebellion to my leadership, etc.... In each case I had no idea what to do. I had no experience to draw from. I had no inner confidence to bolster me. I had no system in place to rely on. I was young, inexperienced, and, to intensify it, people were looking to me. Like he said to Jeremiah, God said to me, "Get behind me and follow me."

> *I am convinced that God is an infinitely better leader than I am follower.*

It is not always easy to follow the Lord's leading. When there are voices shouting at you, from within, from without, and from all around, the Holy Spirit's voice is not always clear. Good choices abound. Sound advice can run in many directions. Godly counsel can differ. I am convinced that God is an infinitely better leader than I am a follower. I will not trust my ability to follow or to hear Him. I will trust that He knows how to lead me and that He will lead me. As a result, so many times after seeking the Lord, I would take a deep breath, pray "Okay, God. I am going to believe this is what you want me to do, stop me if I got it wrong," and stand up to do it with confidence. Of course, it did not always turn out comfortably or even right, but I did move forward without insecurity. My faith was not in my abilities, training, education, or experience, but in a God who was with me.

> When do I get to grow up?
> Actually I hope never.

Inexperience and incompetency drive us to dependency. We always want to be dependent on our Heavenly Father. We never want to believe that we can do it, that we are wise enough, strong enough, experienced enough. We never want to assume that because we have the degrees, the titles, or the years under our belt that we are competent for ministry by ourselves. Remember "we have this treasure in jars of clay, to show that the surpassing power belongs to God and not to us." (2 Corinthians 4:7)

Jeremiah ministered for 40 years in tumultuous and crucial times for God's people. His ministry was effective and long-lasting. I believe it was because of what was established in Jeremiah's first recorded encounter with God.

In that encounter the Lord switches the focus from Jeremiah's inexperience to Himself. We don't know what Jeremiah knew about God. We do know that he was raised in a Levite family so potentially he was taught much about what God is like. It's quite possible that God's words ignited the truth his parents had seeded in him. His young mind, yet to be disillusioned by a cynical world, grabbed hold of who God is. This was solidified by the manifest presence of God touching his mouth. Even with all that, Jeremiah had to still obey and trust that God said was true is actually true.

I have come to accept that God does not tell me to do something that he will not give me the power to do. If He's calling me to enter an uncertain uncomfortable conflict meeting where I know I will be accused, then I can be confident His grace will lubricate any undeserved criticisms. If I have to do a hospital visit and I really don't feel any compassion, then I can obey trusting His Spirit to birth love in my heart. If I sense I need to release an important ministry to someone else's control, then I can do it trusting God will release my heart. If I am called to do something I've never done before, then I will say, "Yes" so I can see God's power at work in me. Whether it's wisdom, stamina, words, compassion, whatever is needed, the Holy Spirit can provide. In reality isn't the entire Christian life beyond us? Isn't everything dependent on the power and presence of God in us? Am I so foolish? Having begun by the Spirit, am I now being perfected by the flesh? (see Galatians 3:3) Unfortunately the older we get, the more experienced we get, the more we might think we can do it ourselves.

After twenty years living in the same neighborhood we stepped out in faith and invited our neighbors for a Christmas party. It was a great night of conversation, getting to know each other, and sharing stories of the neighborhood. I was excited that the door was opening to be friends and to share Jesus. The next day one of them, the father of a boy I coached in baseball, had a heart attack coming home from work and crashed into a tree. He was hospitalized and in a coma. Shocked at first, I quickly saw this as a great opportunity. I went to the hospital to pray over him; I was confident God was going to heal him and his family, the neighbors, my family, and all the baseball community in town would be amazed at God's glory! It was so obvious to me that this was the strategic and right move to make. I would obey and God would show His power.

I did.

He didn't.

I laid my hands on my neighbor's motionless body and prayed. There was no miracle, no sudden change to his vitals, nothing. Neither did anything happen in the days ahead. Instead he died by the end of the week.

I was devastated, "What's wrong with you, God?! This family wanted nothing to do with you before and now they won't either." I was angry, "This was the right move. Why didn't you do something? You're just not strategic!"

The next weekend I was still simmering with unbelief while cooking dinner when there was a knock at our door. It was one of my deceased neighbor's adult sons and he asked, "My mom was wondering if you'd speak at the funeral? We'd like that." Of course, I agreed, but after he left I got on my knees in my kitchen. What I saw as a short sighted and ineffective inaction by God was actually the most strategic decision to be made. I was now going to share Jesus with hundreds of people who would actually sit and listen. People who I had always wanted to talk to, but never had the opportunity. Moreover, in the next three years that same family lost an aunt, a cousin, a grandmother, a mother in law, and the 30 year old son who came to my house that day. Each time they turned to me for the funeral. A family, an entire network of people, who had no faith connection was now hearing about Jesus in their time of need. God was strategic. Despite all my years of experience He knew better. I don't know better. I am still a kid.

We tend to look down on inexperience. We tend to dismiss the comments young people make. We tend to wave off youthful idealism. We tend to ignore the contributions children and teenagers give. We just don't expect much from them. With that way of thinking it's no wonder we don't think much of ourselves when we are young or inexperienced. It's no wonder that insecurity is born when we see ourselves as young or inexperienced. Being a kid, however, is not really a bad thing when you have a Father like Jeremiah's. Instead it forces you to rely on Him!

Jeremiah had such a deep belief in God that he said, "yes" to all God said to say and do. Some tasks were quite unusual. Yet there was a compelling encounter with the Lord that elevated his view of God far above his view of himself. It didn't matter how young, how inexperienced, or how uneducated he was. It would be God at work not Jeremiah.

I don't have to make up for my inexperience with an exaggerated self-confidence. I don't have to compensate for my youthfulness with defensiveness. I don't have to replace my insecurity with an aura of bravado and toughness. I don't have to counteract my self-doubt with more control. No, my Daddy is bigger than anything. He's smarter, wiser, more experienced, more strategic, more loving than I am or could ever be. He's king of all kings.

FOR YOUR OWN REFLECTION:

1. How do you respond when a position or viewpoint you hold is challenged? Do you take it personally? Are you stubborn, belligerent, defensive, or argumentative?

2. What is your first reaction to attempting something risky or uncertain?

3. What might be the difference between ministering out of your incompetence versus out of your competence?

4. How can your greatest strength be your greatest weakness?

5. What is it about God that makes Him so much greater than you?

10

Paul: Finding Grace in Your Weakness

"Deny your weakness, and you will never realize God's strength in you."
- Joni Eareckson Tada

    I get the impression from some Christians that the Apostle Paul is considered a Hercules, a demi-god, not a mere mortal like us. His faith was superhuman and his deeds legendary. His ministries were Midas touched. His church plants were all sustainable and long lasting. He could convince any jury whether the glove fit or not. His teachings and his life were impeccable. Even Peter was corrected by him. This guy had it all together! As much as we look to emulate him, deep down many of us feel that just might be impossible.

    As my family sat down in Cinemark to watch the new *Sherlock Holmes* movie, I felt a wave of fear overcome me. I felt claustrophobic, confined, trapped in my seat. Suddenly I was at war within myself. I wanted to run outside. Emotional klaxons were sounding in my body that danger was nearby, but my mind was saying there wasn't any danger.

    "What's wrong with me? Am I going crazy?"

    During that time I wondered at my ability to be a pastor; self-doubt compounded my emotional state. In that time a particular verse struck me from the life of the Apostle Paul. "For even when we came into Macedonia our flesh had no rest, but we were afflicted on every side: conflicts without, fears within." (2 Corinthians 7:5 NASB) Herculean Paul admitted to an internal weakness, a war within, and the opponent was fear. That prompted me to examine his life through a slightly different lens. What I began to see was no superhero, but a mortal plagued with fears, anxieties, temptations, and insecurities.

    I now believe Paul wrestled with insecurity. Consider these observations of Paul's life:

- He was wrong about God and the Messiah for years. He was so convinced of his view that he killed for it!
- He saw himself as the worst sinner (1 Timothy 1:15).
- He lived in constant uncertainty and danger. He was beaten, shipwrecked, imprisoned, threatened by riots, falsely accused, all the while traveling without any guaranteed job or hotel reservations.
- He had a physical ailment (Galatians 4:13).
- He was an unskilled public speaker (2 Corinthians 11:6).
- He had an unspecified issue he called a "thorn in the flesh" (2 Corinthians 12).
- He was so overwhelmed that he despaired of living and wanted to give up (2 Corinthians 1:8).

These could easily be ripe for the breeding of insecurity. There's the emotional regret and grief of the past, inadequacy for the present, and anxiety for the future. Clearly Paul saw himself as weak. Previously I only saw the beginning and end of Paul's sanctification journey; what I overlooked was the process in between where a real man experienced the same emotions I do today. Self-doubt receded when I recognized this. Now my search was for what helped Paul. What kept him from internal defeat? What kept him from being consumed with fear? What kept him from being driven to avoid failure? How did he deal with all this insecurity?

Anxiety is a messy subject. We are complex beings with a spiritual, emotional, and physical side to us. Consequently some severe cases of anxiety are not simply wiped away by memorizing verses or conjuring up more faith. For example, when Elijah ran away in anxiety and even had suicidal thoughts, God's initial help was to give him sleep and physical nourishment (see 1 Kings 19). God then manifested His presence to Elijah, spoke encouragement, and provided a partner. Therefore, it is not my intent to give a definitive treatise on anxiety or to provide only "spiritual" solutions to it. Exercise, nutrition, and rest are God's design for our lives, as well, but by themselves they are limited in dealing with the deep insecurities ruminating in our hearts.

Most of us have been directed to Paul's words in Philippians 4:6-8 for dealing with anxiety. "Do not be anxious about anything, but in every situation, by prayer and petition, with thanksgiving, present your requests to God. And the peace of God, which transcends all understanding, will guard your hearts and your minds in Christ Jesus." We assume the remedy is prayer. And we are right ... well, almost.

I am convinced the verses that precede the popular text open up another dimension to our prayer. "Rejoice in the Lord always. I will say it again: Rejoice! Let your gentleness be evident to all. The Lord is near." Many commentaries take the phrase "The Lord is near" as referring to His second coming. In other words, don't let all this stuff worry you because Jesus is coming back soon. Okay, but what if we take the phrase as near in space instead of near in time (Robertson's Word Pictures of the New Testament). Interestingly the ancient Greek translation of the Old Testament, the Septuagint, translates the same phrase in Psalms 119:151 in the sense of presence, not of coming. An older translation catches this alternative flavor: "Delight yourselves in God, yes, find your joy in him at all times. Have a reputation for gentleness, and never forget the nearness of your Lord." (Philippians 4:4-5 J.B. PHILLIPS) I get the impression then that Paul is saying to enjoy an intimacy with the Lord. Be aware of His presence in your life. Look for Him. Position yourself to see and hear Him. Cultivate your senses to be aware of Him.

Sure enough we read of God demonstrating His presence at keys points in Paul's life. Of course, we know that Jesus appears at his conversion in Acts 9. Then, the Spirit clearly speaks to the Antioch church leaders to send Paul on his missionary journeys. After crossing over to Europe, running from persecution in Thessalonica, dodging abusers in Berea, and debating philosophers in Athens, Paul faces tough opposition in Corinth. It does not appear that this mission into the new areas is turning out so well. Then, the Lord appears to Paul in a supernatural way, "Do not be afraid, but go on speaking and do not be silent, for I am with you, and no one will attack you to harm you, for I have many in this city who are my people." (Acts 18:9-10) He then stays in Corinth for 18 months, the longest of his stops in Europe. Fast forward 8 years or so and Paul is on a ship heading for Rome when a storm threatens to sink the vessel. An angel of the Lord appears to him, "Do not be afraid, Paul; you must stand before Caesar. And behold, God has granted you all those who sail with you." (Acts 27:24) New beginnings. New situations. New transitions. Each event seems to occur at a moment when insecurity could be the strongest.

Personally I have had three distinct and clear supernatural manifestations of God's presence. There have been hundreds of others, but these three stand out and buttress my soul. The first happened before getting married when there was great uncertainty, fear, and insecurity. The second was just before we launched our first church plant; again, it was a time of fear and uncertainty. The third was when I was transitioning to my new role and my daughter was suffering with mental illness. Anxiety, depression, and uncertainty were riddling my body when God manifested His presence. In all three cases, I was pursuing God and positioning myself to be aware of His presence.

There is no person on earth I would rather be with than my wife. She is my best friend, my confidant, my partner in ministry, and my lover. Knowing that my love language is physical touch, she made a fun resolution this year. She would kiss me every day. Not just a peck or a hello kiss, but a real long KISS. For me, that is a tremendously intimate moment of my day! I cannot wait for that time of the day, but I don't know when she's going to kiss me. Moreover if I don't ever spend time with her, or if I ignore her when she walks into my office, or if I walk away when she comes close, or if I stay out all the time playing sports with my buddies, then I will miss out on that intimacy. It's the same in my relationship with God. I want to position myself to experience Him. I want to be present with Him so He will really be present with me. Like James says, "Draw near to God, and he will draw near to you." (James 4:4)

Let me take the analogy further.

How would I respond if someone other than my wife tried to kiss me that way? What if that person was ugly by my standards? What if I thought person was coming toward me to hurt me? I would be disgusted and pull back. I would avoid that person as much as I could. Many people have that reaction to God for any number of reasons:

- Religious caricatures of a judgmental distant God.
- Wounds caused by significant others.
- Disillusionment with God's purposes.
- Disappointment at life's circumstances.
- Anger at God's seeming inaction.

These tend to cloud our understanding of God. He looks ugly and dangerous; why would I let him get close?

Paul pursued intimacy with God because he saw himself as weak and God still wanted him. He was wrong and God still wanted him. He was sick and God still wanted him. He was broken and messed up, yet God still wanted him. He was the ugly one. He was the dangerous one. And God wanted him close.

His pursuit, then, came out of a recognition of how weak he actually was. He didn't see himself as strong, courageous, beautiful, or worthy. Even when he boasted in 2 Corinthians 11-12, his bragging culminated in his admission of weakness! To which God's response is to provide even more grace. "'My grace is sufficient for you, for my power is made perfect in weakness.' Therefore I will boast all the more gladly of my weaknesses, so that the power of Christ may rest upon me. For the sake of Christ, then, I am content with weaknesses, insults, hardships, persecutions, and calamities. For when I am weak, then I am strong." (2 Corinthians 12:9-10)

The flow of Romans 7-8 also lends itself to this. He was trapped, exhausted, and hopeless when he cries out, "What a wretched man I am! Who will rescue me from this body of death?" (Romans 7:24) Paul is giving up. "I've tried everything and nothing helps. I'm at the end of my rope." His willpower is shattered. His strength sapped. His confidence broken. Paul was a mess, entangled in his own inadequacies and failures. He tried and tried and tried and still ended up failing, unable to break the power of the sin nature in his daily life.

How many times have you heard the condemning voices from those in your church?

"I ruined my marriage. What's the use of going on."
"I'm a loser; God can't use me."
"I fell again; I guess I'm just not a good Christian."
"I just can't let others see me like this; I'm ashamed."
"Why would God want me back?"

Our self-condemning thoughts bring guilt and shame, insecurity and fear. For some it causes the abandonment of relationships and a hiding from others. For example, after giving a workshop on mentoring, a pastor came up to me afterward to talk. He admitted that he had a difficult time mentoring anyone. As we talked it became clear that he had been hurt by those in his church over the years. Slowly over the years he put up protective shields around his heart and had pulled away from people.

Imagine if my wife came toward me one day and I thought it was going to be that KISS, but instead she slapped me. She verbally berated me for my failures. She pointed out all the things I hadn't done for her over the years. I would certainly pull away from her. I would also probably distance myself from her emotionally. Our relationship would become quite utilitarian - what you can do for me. Such is how many people react to God. Not only do they see him as ugly and dangerous, but that he will only point out their failures and make them feel even worse. That is exactly what He does not do to Paul (or any of us). Immediately following his admission of failure, Paul brings us to the truth that we're not condemned, we're not hopeless cases, we're not losers. "There is now no condemnation for those in Christ Jesus." (Romans 8:1) Basically God says, "Yes, you are a mess and I am not angry with you."

Paul goes on in Romans 8 demonstrating God's grace for his weakness. The first grace or provision for Paul's weakness is the Holy Spirit (Romans 8:1-11). The Holy Spirit empowers us as we position ourselves ("set your mind") for His presence. He does what we cannot do. He brings genuine ministry success. He fuels the movement we desire. He accomplishes the work of the Father. He is the power we need to be successful.

The second provision is a new identity as sons (Romans 8:12-17). Paul uses the term Abba or Daddy to illustrate the intimacy we are invited into with the Heavenly Father. Embracing sonship is crucial for pursuing intimacy. Sonship puts our hearts at rest when God comes close to us. We are accepted into God's family. We belong. We are nurtured, cared for, and enjoyed by a Father who wants us.

The third provision is the security of God's love (Romans 8:18-35). He makes it clear that nothing is going to change God's mind about us. He is not fickle in his love, one minute liking us, the next slapping us. He is constant and continual amidst life's uncertainties and chaos. He stabilizes our anxieties, calms our fears, and controls all we cannot.

That's the one Paul wanted to be close to.

In the same way, God is passionate for me. He provides power for my success. He accepts me as his son. He guarantees my security for all of eternity.

He's the dad I never had.

He's the dad who is present.

He's the dad who invites me into his workshop and doesn't get upset when I mess up his projects.

He's the dad who disciplines gently and lovingly for my own benefit.

He's the dad who enjoys me.

He's the dad who's proud of me.

He's the dad who I don't have to hide the report card from.

He's the dad who is powerful enough for my weakness.

Now THAT is a dad I want to come closer to me.

FOR YOUR OWN REFLECTION:

1. What happens in you when a weakness of yours is made known to you? ... to others?

2. What about yourself do you think God doesn't like?

3. How is being "liked" by God different to you than being "loved" by Him?

4. What does it mean to you to be a son?

5. What experiences have you had with God as father that might have shaped you to not see His passion for you?

11

How The Gospel Deals With Insecurity

Frank is a tough looking church planter. He is burly, bald, tattooed, and a former gang member. Since I am a small guy, I wouldn't want to meet him in a dark alley! Yet there is something about his demeanor that is just plain "guy cool." One day for our coaching appointment, he rolled up on his Harley. As he pulled off his military like helmet, I strolled over and asked if I could sit on his bike. He said, "Sure," and like a little kid I tried to get my little body on the massive machine. I finally did only to scorch my bare leg on the exhaust pipes! As I cringed in pain, Frank chuckled, looked at the bad burns, and said nonchalantly, "You'll be fine." Not wanting to be seen as a wimp I spent our lunch with the ice water glass on my leg trying to imagine it didn't hurt. Maybe I thought for a brief moment that I could be like Frank. Try as hard as I can, I cannot be Frank. He is a unique man. A special creation. A one of kind handcrafted masterpiece. We do, however, have one huge thing in common. Our maker is the same.

Artists, craftsmen, authors, musicians, chefs, directors all have a signature on their creations. It might be a literal signature or initials, a certain font, a style, a pattern, lighting, etc.... Something that denotes it is their work. Something that will distinguish their work from someone else's or even from a forgery. Frank and I, every human being for that matter, have the signature of God on us. Scripture refers to it as the "image" and "likeness" of God. Rather than repeat volumes of systematic theological discussions, let me just point out one aspect that I believe is important. "It is not good for man to be alone" (Genesis 2:18) indicates to me that we were designed as relational beings. The Triune God existing in eternal relationship placed the stamp of relationship upon his prime creation. The Father, Son, and Holy Spirit exist and function in perfect relationship, in perfect love.

We were fully loved in the Garden. Our souls were flooded with love. His presence provided all the love we ever needed. We had intimacy with Him. We were important to Him. We were safe with Him. Our identity was based on that love relationship with God. This kind of love is not the fickle, romantic, emotion-based stuff society peddles today. It is genuine, sacrificial, unconditional, divine. It is love that satisfies the deepest longings of the human heart. What are these? From the early church fathers of the 3rd century to Saint Ignatius of Loyola in the 16th century to modern psychology and leadership books three common longings, motivations, passions, or drives always emerge: belonging, mattering, safety, or as I have come to explain them - to be accepted, to be significant, to be secure.

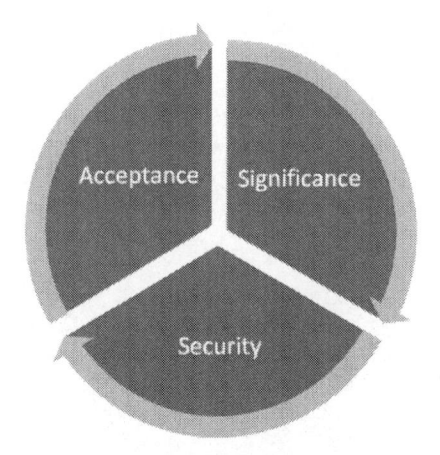

(Diagram: a circle divided into three sections labeled "Acceptance", "Significance", and "Security", with arrows flowing around the circle.)

Have you ever felt so comfortable with a person that just being with them is relaxing? For me it's when my wife cuddles with me. When she curls up next to me in bed and puts her arm on my chest, I can feel the tension ease out of my body. I feel calm. I feel accepted by her. I am important to her. I am safe with nothing to hide. This is what Adam and Eve had with God in the Garden. These three things were ours back in the beginning.

We were fully accepted. God hung out with us. He enjoyed spending time with us. We were declared good.

We were wholly significant. Important. Vital. We held a special place in creation. We were given responsibility to care for his creation.

We were completely secure. Safe. The Garden was set apart from the wild world. No natural disasters, no harmful diseases, no death, no carnivorous beasts, no blood sucking ticks. We were close to God and under his protection. We experienced God's love by being accepted by him, being deemed significant by him, and being kept. Our souls were bathed in God's love. He Himself was present.

BUT we all know what happened. The serpent said to the woman, "You will not surely die. For God knows that when you eat of it your eyes will be opened, and you will be like God, knowing good and evil." So when the woman saw that the tree was good for food, and that it was a delight to the eyes, and that the tree was to be desired to make one wise, she took of its fruit and ate, and she also gave some to her husband who was with her, and he ate. (Genesis 3:4-6)

We broke that relationship with God. Basically Adam & Eve thought "I don't want to be dependent on God." "I want to decide for myself what's good or bad, right or wrong." "I want to do it my way." "I want to be in control!" As a result, our relationship with God was severed. All the feelings of acceptance, significance, and security are replaced by shame, guilt, and failure. The supply of love to our souls was cut off.

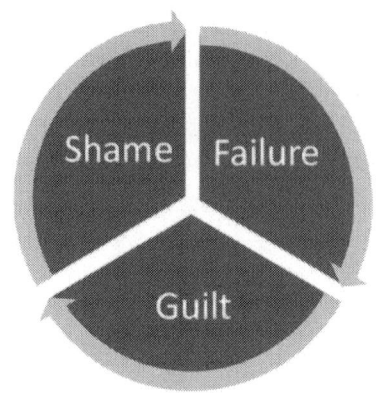

So what do we do? We strive to feel that which we lost. We demand to be loved. We manipulate and use people to get what we need. We seek love any way we can. We look for alternative pleasures and people and plans to experience that which is now lacking in our souls. We engage in an endless pursuit of success. We juggle relationships to make sure everyone likes us. We arrange life and manage people so we are in control. All of our loving is tainted, ruined, contaminated. Our souls desperately try to supply that which is lacking. Because our souls are messed up, our behavior is also. Even when our behavior is not overtly bad, it's motivated by something other than love. This is the story of the human race. This is the story of every human being. This is my story and your story.

The Gospel makes it possible now for this to be reversed. Jesus Christ restores us. He does it by giving us that which we lost - love. A classic Pauline declaration of our salvation is founded on love. But God, being rich in mercy, because of the great love with which he loved us, even when we were dead in our trespasses, made us alive together with Christ—by grace you have been saved— and raised us up with him and seated us with him in the heavenly places in Christ Jesus, so that in the coming ages he might show the immeasurable riches of his grace in kindness toward us in Christ Jesus. For by grace you have been saved through faith. And this is not your own doing; it is the gift of God, not a result of works, so that no one may boast. (Ephesians 2:4-9) The pipeline to God's love has been reopened by the sacrificial death of Christ, itself the penultimate act of love. In Christ I am once again fully loved - accepted, significant, secure.

THE GOSPEL EXPOSES UNBELIEF

As loved as I now am in Christ, I don't always FEEL that way. We do not always experience this reality. We do not automatically feel accepted, significant, and secure. We do not suddenly become angelic do-gooders. We do not magically begin loving everyone from a pure heart and a clean conscience. The residue of leftover sin, the wounds caused by others, the calluses of years of living for self, and the lies of society and Satan constipate the emotional reality of the love we truly have.

When my oldest son was 9 years old, he would often say or do something disrespectful that would get me very angry. My wife pointed out, however, that the small amount of disrespect he gave me was met by an avalanche of anger. It was incongruent, unwarranted, and unbalanced. One day after one tirade she astutely asked, "Do you remember another time you felt this way?" Immediately the Spirit brought to mind times when I never felt respected by my dad. I will never forget the revelation that happened that day. I had been responding not to the present, but to the past. Because my earthly father did not make me feel significant to him I was limited in embracing my heavenly Father's love and hence blocked in giving love to my son.

How can what a 9 year old or a 30 year old dad say trump what the Almighty God of the universe declares? It sounds ludicrous, yet so many of us live like this.

It really shouldn't shock us when we read Paul's prayer for the Ephesians. For this reason I bow my knees before the Father, from whom every family in heaven and on earth is named, that according to the riches of his glory he may grant you to be strengthened with power through his Spirit in your inner being, so that Christ may dwell in your hearts through faith—that you, being rooted and grounded in love, may have strength to comprehend with all the saints what is the breadth and length and height and depth, and to know the love of Christ that surpasses knowledge, that you may be filled with all the fullness of God. (Ephesians 3:14-19) I doubt he would have prayed this if those in his day were not struggling with embracing the love of God.

One leader shared with me his struggle with being genuinely accepted by God. He spent his youth locked out of groups, rejected, and as a self-perceived loser. As a Christian he believed God accepted him despite being a loser. What God did for him was tell him, "You're way better than you see yourself." It wasn't God sadly accepting a loser, but God accepting him for himself. As the Spirit revealed the Father's love to him, his view of himself, of God, and of others was updated to a newer version that ran on the operating system of being fully and completely loved.

Most would agree that our thinking (our belief systems, world view, values, etc...) affects the choices we make, the behaviors we choose, and even our emotional state. It is hard to ignore the significance of Scriptures like:

- "Do not be conformed to this world, but be transformed by the renewal of your MIND, that by testing you may discern what is the will of God, what is good and acceptable and perfect." (Romans 12:2)
- "For the weapons of our warfare are not of the flesh but have divine power to destroy strongholds. We destroy arguments and every lofty opinion raised against the knowledge of God,

and take every THOUGHT captive to obey Christ." (2 Corinthians 10:4-5)
- "Finally, brothers, whatever is true, whatever is honorable, whatever is just, whatever is pure, whatever is lovely, whatever is commendable, if there is any excellence, if there is anything worthy of praise, THINK about these things." (Philippians 4:8)

It is, however, not as simple as a new plug and play device for our computers. I have spent and will probably continue to spend my entire adult life uncovering false beliefs and exposing misaligned purposes.

Recently a pastor shared with me how negative his self-talk is. With tears in his eyes he told me he calls himself "stupid" and "a failure" anytime something goes wrong ... including a minor project in his garage. His self-talk exposed what he really believed about himself. He recognized that this in turn made him insecure in his leadership, propelled to not let others down, and fearful of taking risks. The Spirit was uncovering false beliefs and showing how they tainted his purposes and motivations. Now, he was responding with repentance.

THE GOSPEL CHANGES WHO WE ARE

Let me explain it another way along the lines of who we are now. We saw in the last chapter that one of God's provision for Paul's weakness was a new identity as a son. "For all who are led by the Spirit of God are sons of God. For you did not receive the spirit of slavery to fall back into fear, but you have received the spirit of adoption as sons, by whom we cry, "Abba! Father!"" (Romans 8:12-15). God declares us to be his very own sons (and daughters). The Gospel gives us a new identity. We are adopted into God's family. One of the pastors I work with has adopted multiple children. He shared with me how surprised he was when he got their legal birth certificates from the government. They listed him and his wife as parents and looked exactly the same as his biological children's birth certificates. There was no difference at all. There was no indication that they were anything less than his biological children. They were completely and utterly his. No questions.

In between ministries I led painting crews during the summer in a local school. My crews were made up of high school students who needed summer jobs. Each crew was usually separated from the others and distributed throughout the high school painting various rooms and halls. I would float between them supervising, giving instruction, or making sure they had what supplies they needed. Without fail when I showed up, the teenagers scrambled into high gear making sure I saw them working hard. They were afraid of the boss. They worked out of fear. Paul would say they were slaves.

Jack Frost in his book *Spiritual Slavery to Spiritual Sonship* puts it this way, "We either live our life feeling safe, secure and at rest in Father's heart, experiencing His love and giving it away, or we live our life with apprehension and uncertainty, struggling constantly with the fear of trusting, the fear of rejection, and the fear of opening up our heart to love—the three fears common to all people." When we are not living in our standing as sons, then we live in fear always trying to please others, ourselves, or God. When we do not experience our adoption, then we drive ourselves in fear to perform and prove ourselves. What we measure may be different than the next person, but we all do it.

Slaves must work and perform to secure their worth in the world. Slaves are always striving for belonging, importance, and safety. Slaves live in perpetual insecurity, uncertainty, and dependence on others' opinions of them. This was the issue for both sons in the Prodigal Son story. The younger figured he had to come back as a slave because he had been so bad to his dad while the older defined himself by how hard he worked for his dad. Both missed out on what it meant to be a son. Sons have a special place with their dad. They share in all the dad has. They remind themselves daily that they're fully loved by their father. Sons recognize that they are accepted, significant, and secure, and that nothing they can do or not do changes that. God's sons (and daughters) know who they are because their identity is cemented by what Jesus has done for them.

My wife says that I am an "out of sight, out of mind" guy. In other words, I don't usually keep up with friends who move away. In a recent conversation with our youngest son who just graduated college, she mentioned that to him. His response was both encouraging and insightful. "Oh no, I might be out of sight, but I know I am on dad's mind. He's there when I need him." He's right. If my sons or daughter call, I will pick up the phone; I recognize the number. On the other hand, if a former parishioner calls, I will probably not pick up; I won't recognize the number and sometimes not even the name! Sons and daughters have a special place in a dad's mind. They are not workers, not servants, not church members, not employees; they are family, all the time, everywhere.

I have discovered that the pressure to be perfect is released when I stop striving to prove myself and rest in the undeserved gift Jesus provides for me. On the other hand, when I am not convinced of God's love I work hard to feel accepted by appeasing others, or to feel significant by making a name for myself, or to feel secure by exercising control over circumstances and people.. As a result, when I am rejected, fail, or am proved wrong, I react with anger, depression, numbing myself, or simply by trying harder. After thirty five years I have seen these as dashboard warning lights. I know something is amiss within me when any of these happens. I know I am not believing truth.

> **The Gospel isn't just for unbelievers. It isn't just about getting me into heaven.**

What the author of Hebrews writes might apply, "So then, there remains a Sabbath rest for the people of God, for whoever has entered God's rest has also rested from his works as God did from his." (Hebrews 4:9-10) Those in the past missed out on God's rest. God's rest was obviously the Promised Land, but it was also the place of God's abundant provision. We could even see it as a state of trusting and living in God's provision. Israel missed out because they didn't believe what God said. Instead they wandered and lived in the wilderness. They decided to meet their needs apart from God; they chose to keep on working, striving, and trying harder to prove their worth. They could not rest. Unbelief kept them from experiencing their full identity as the nation of God. In the same way, unbelief keeps me from experiencing God's provision of love.

I wrote in my journal recently, "If I am living out of a state of rest, then it's okay to fail, to be wrong, to be corrected, to have someone not like me, to have an issue left unresolved, to take risks, to do something I've never done before or don't feel competent at, or to be vulnerable. I don't have to be successful, to be right, to be well liked, to have all tension gone. God provided for my standing with him so I don't have to earn it."

THE GOSPEL REMINDS US WHO GOD IS

Let me explain it a third way along the lines of who God is. In Tim Chester's book *You Can Change* he brings forth four liberating truths about God. He suggests that underlying many of our struggles is a failure to believe one of these truths at a functional level. Just like the warnings in the book of Hebrews say, unbelief lies behind our sins and prevents us from resting in the love of God.

> **GOD IS GREAT** - Job's story leads him to the inescapable conclusion that God is sovereign. He intricately designed the universe. He wonderfully formed each one of us. His plan trumps all others. His purposes cannot be thwarted. His ways are not my ways. As a finite created being, my power is quite limited. I want to be in control, to avoid pain, to accomplish a better more blessed life for myself and those I love. BUT control is merely an illusion. God is great so I don't need to be in control.
>
> **GOD IS GLORIOUS** - The word "glory" carries with it the idea of weight, of importance, of magnitude. God is weighty or heavy. Everything else shrinks in comparison to Him. Consequently what He thinks is paramount. His opinion carries infinite weight. It is what He considers important that is important. Yet as a needy finite being, I long for others' approval. I want them to be happy with me. I want to impress them. Their opinion matters to me. I want to avoid rejection. BUT their view of me is never accurate. God is glorious so I don't have to be fearful of anyone.
>
> **GOD IS GOOD** - After created everything, God said "It is good." The inherent goodness of creation comes from the nature of the Creator. He is good and he designed his creation to function best in connection with Himself. As a result the creation is needy. We have a need for food, drink, rest, love, relationship. Meanwhile, He is Yahweh - the self-sufficient

One, the all-sufficient; He has no needs. He Himself is all creation needs. As a needy created being, I fend for my own needs. I arrange my life to meet my needs. Hunger, thirst, intimacy, and relationship become driving forces in my life. BUT they never fully satisfy, they never quench the deeper need of my soul. God is good so I don't have to look elsewhere for satisfaction or pleasure.

GOD IS GRACIOUS - The story of God is a narrative of grace. God created us and pursued relationship with us. We rebelled and chose to live independent of God. Nonetheless God continued to pursue us by sending a Savior to forgive us. Despite our best efforts to ignore Him, He continues to pursue and restore all of His creation to what He originally intended. As an imperfect flawed being I spend my life trying to prove my worth, my value, my contribution. I yearn to be important. I strive to be perfect. I try hard to earn love and forgiveness. BUT nothing we do is ever enough. God is gracious so I don't have to prove myself to me, to others, or to God.

One day as I bathed in these truths of who God is, I took it further.

- God is omniscient, so I don't have to know everything.
- God is eternal, so I don't have to be in a rush.
- God is omnipresent, so I don't have to be afraid of being abandoned.
- God is merciful so I don't have to feel bad about asking for something for myself.
- God is faithful so I don't have to worry about the future.

Taking the attributes of God beyond a mere list of qualities to personalize them has done wonders for my heart. Daily I remind myself of who God is. Recently I wrote them on my whiteboard wall so I can reflect on them at a glance.

Insecurity expresses itself in all shapes and sizes, in all personality types, and in all generations. That is because insecurity is rooted in the brokenness of humanity. When we are separated from our creator we have nothing but ourselves and that is frightening. The

Gospel is God's answer to our brokenness. It is not just a "forgive my sins" transaction, rather there is far more to the Gospel that deeply affects who we are. It is the basis for the Holy Spirit changing us.

> What do we do?
> How do we implement the truth of the Gospel?
> That's what I want to explore in my final chapter.

FOR YOUR OWN REFLECTION:

1. Which of the three - significance, security, or acceptance - do you tend to strive for the most? How does that express itself in your life, behavior, or relationships?

2. What would it take for Jesus to free you to experience His provision in all three?

3. How does unbelief creep into your life? What false beliefs do you have about God, about yourself?

4. Take some time to meditate over the attributes of God. Reflect on the implications for your own heart. For each write it out in this format - God is _____ so I don't have to _____.

12

Catalyst For Change

If there is nothing new under the sun, but that which
Has been before, how are our brains cheated,
Which, toiling to create something new, mistakenly
Brings forth something that already exists
- Shakespeare's Sonnet 59 plain English paraphrase

As I sat in Starbucks writing this book, my wife slipped up behind me and said in my ear, "I'm so proud of you for fulfilling a dream to write a book."

I looked up at her, "Thanks, but I'm not fulfilling a dream, I'm obeying a command."

For decades people encouraged me to write a book, but I didn't think I had anything new to share. There were so many books out there that every topic seemed to be covered. Nowadays with the proliferation of the internet and e-books, everyone is writing a book! What's new to say? As a result, this is not about a new truth or a new formula or some new theology. No, it's simply my journey of continually applying the ointment of God's truth so that it permeates deeper than the epidermis of my life. It is my story of applying the recurring truth of the gospel to ever deepening and widening areas of my life. What God showed me over the years was not something new, but something old which is to be continually renewed and repeated.

The church at Colosse was tempted to look for new truths. Situated along a trade route they were exposed to many religions, sects, and alternative philosophies. Visiting teachers were offering special knowledge and supposedly deeper truths. The more they heard, the more they began to drift toward "new" ways of spirituality - spiritism, angel worship, ancestral worship, asceticism, traditionalism, ritualism, rigid rules and regulations, and basically self-help techniques. Paul in his letter to them focuses on bringing them back to the real thing. Forget the substitutes. The convenience, low cost, and attractiveness of substitute options do not truly transform lives. Instead, it's back to the beginning. "So then, just as you received Christ Jesus as Lord, continue to live your lives in him" (Colossians 2:6).

How did we receive this person, Jesus Christ?

Well, it was not by magical self-help formulas, the accumulation of knowledge, determined will power, religious rituals, or earning his favor. It was by grace through faith. We first entered the Christian life by recognizing we are not good enough for God. We continue growing by constantly exposing the lies and unbelief that bind and blind our hearts and minds. We admit them for what they are. It is still by grace through faith.

The activator of God's transformative grace in our lives is still faith. The catalyst for God's power is belief. Israel missed out on God's promises because of unbelief. Hebrews 4 extended that example to all who miss out of God's provision. Unbelief is behind our sin, our problems, our brokenness. We don't really believe that God is good enough, strong enough, or caring enough. This is the gospel. We cannot do anything for ourselves. God, on the other hand, can. We embrace Him and trust Him.

For me, I began recognizing that the gospel is not just for unbelievers. The gospel isn't just about getting me into Christianity. It is to be repeatedly applied over and over throughout my life. I don't have a willpower problem or a discipline problem or a knowledge problem, I have a belief problem. I am not really trusting God for who He really is and what he says about me. The match that ignites true change in my life is faith in the living Christ.

For years people told me that I was a good speaker and teacher. No matter what feedback I received on Sundays, I just did not believe I was. I was stuck in insecurity. Then one Sunday after preaching I stepped off the platform and a very strong impression came over me. "You are good. I have gifted you. Now, trust me for it." From that day onward I saw myself as a good speaker; I am no longer insecure and worried about my public speaking. What I believe about myself, what I believe about God is crucial for loosening the paralysis of insecurity.

Since the gospel frees me, the next question is how do I position myself to experience this freedom at different levels in my life?

It was the evening of Oct. 13, 2001, the seventh inning of the third game of the American League Division Series between the Yankees and Athletics when Derek Jeter made his iconic "flip play." The throw from the outfield had sailed over the cut off men to where Jeter caught it and backhand flipped it to the catcher for the out. It was an amazing play that was never seen before. What's even more amazing is that Derek was actually in the right position because the team practiced it. He was in position to receive the throw to get the out to preserve the lead to secure the victory.

I have to ask myself, am I in the right position to receive the throw from God?

I saw in the lives of Moses, Joshua, David, Jeremiah, and Paul that when we engage with and experience the person, the power, the presence, and the people of God insecurity begins to lose its hold over us. As a result, these four positions have emerged as vital to my own journey.

POSITIONED FOR HIS PRESENCE

We all know that God is everywhere, but there are times we KNOW God is right here. A. W. Tozer drew the distinction in his classic *The Pursuit of God*:

> The Presence and the manifestation of the Presence are not the same. There can be the one without the other. God is here when we are wholly unaware of it. He is manifest only when and as we are aware of His Presence. On our part there must be surrender to the Spirit of God, for His work it is to show us the Father and the Son. If we co-operate with Him in loving obedience God will manifest Himself to us, and that manifestation will be the difference between a nominal Christian life and a life radiant with the light of His face.[1]

It was drilled into me from my initial years as a believer to spend daily time with God. At first it was sweet and new to me, but later it became the badge of being a good Christian. Daily devotions, quiet times, personal Bible study, Scripture memory and times of prayer are great, but they are not the end or the goal. There are really good things that can distract us from experiencing His presence. When we see them, however, as mere pointers, as what we do to position ourselves to meet with God, then they have a proper place.

Let me draw the distinction this way. I can buy flowers for my wife, make reservations at a nice restaurant, get tickets to a show, and set up a romantic candlelit atmosphere for afterward, but if I spend the entire time checking my voice mail, texts and emails rather than engaging with her, then I have not experienced her. I may be doing all the right things, but there's no intimacy.

When I started my first church I started each Monday by going to a nearby park to just be alone with God. Rather than be consumed by all the feedback from Sunday or rushed to start all the things needed to be done that week, I would get alone with God. It was probably the most important thing I did in starting that church. I would have been overwhelmed by the needs, the complaints, the problems, and the conflicts if I did not make that a habit of my ministry. Sometimes it didn't feel like anything special, sometimes God's presence was obvious, but most of the time it was simply encouraging and strengthening.

For me, it wasn't a matter of doing the right thing, but of engaging with my Father on a relational level. This is why understanding my sonship is so important. If I am trying to prove myself to God, then I tend to ramp up the activity and get things done so I don't get in trouble. If I am striving to earn His favor, then my motives are skewed and I'm just fulfilling an obligation. If I am confident as a son, then I can approach Him without shame, without fear. I can rest, I can enjoy His gift of Sabbath.

Over the years I have added other ways to position myself for God's presence besides a daily time alone with God. I have practiced some Biblical meditation, spent time worshipping along with Youtube videos, taken midday naps listening to the Bible, used liturgical prayers and confessions, and set aside times of silence, solitude, and stillness. None of these is a magic formula; they are simply ways for me to be aware of God's presence and receive what He might have for me at that moment.

Sometimes what He has for me does not fit into the paradigm of what I am familiar or comfortable with. Since I was trained in a non-charismatic setting, I have had to learn to be open to what some would say is supernatural. Coincidences are no longer random accidents, but something I have to consider as coming from God. The thoughts that pop into my head at no prompting of my own, the Scripture that I am suddenly reminded of, the song that I wake up humming, and the images that appear in my mind's eye when praying for someone may very well be a manifestation of God's Spirit, of His presence. Whether we call them "prophetic" or "the voice of God" or simply impressions from God doesn't matter. God is demonstrating the reality that He is present. I want to be ready for that. I want to be in position to receive.

POSITIONED FOR HIS PERSON

There are so many ministry help books available. Everything is dissected, analyzed, and explained. It's like church growth has become a sabermetric sport! In my first years of pastoring I was inundated with books about how to do ministry. After 10+ years of reading so many I finally gave up. I committed to a year hiatus from all ministry related books; I would read only devotional books or those about the person of God. I was weary from good ideas, expectations, and an abundance of strategies.

A key verse for me was, "And this is eternal life, that they know you the only true God, and Jesus Christ whom you have sent." (John 17:3) I was not saved to produce or perform. I was saved to know a person. I was not saved to accumulate Biblical knowledge since Jesus declared himself to be the truth (see John 14:6). Paul was one of the most theologically educated and ministry trained men of his day, but he considered it worth "crap" compared to knowing the person of Jesus (See Philippines 3).

How well do I know God?
What is He like?
What are the implications of who He is and what He's like?

It's no wonder taking the attributes of God beyond a mere list of qualities to personalizing them has done wonders for my heart. One way I have enjoyed doing this is through musical praise and worship.

In the second year of my first church plant I took my worship leader to a worship conference. It was not just contemporary in style but also quite charismatic in theology and presentation. At that time in our lives we were both a little uncomfortable especially when the teacher made it seem like disobedience if we didn't raise our hands when singing. The night before the next session we made a pact - neither of us would succumb to manipulation and raise our hands. The next day, however, I was so emotionally absorbed in worship that I raised my hands. My friend looked over at one point and, to this day, jokes that I abandoned and betrayed him! I was so focused on God that pleasing my friend lost its importance.

When I read the Scriptures about who God is, my mind is illuminated and I am intellectually engaged. When my life is devoted in service and sacrifice, I am physically and volitionally engaged. When I praise God with singing I am emotionally engaged. It's no wonder that "psalms and hymns and spiritual songs, singing and making melody to the Lord with your heart" are connected with being filled with the Spirit (Ephesians 5:18-19). Music directed to the Lord has a spiritual and psychological benefit. For me it connects what I believe with how I feel. It bridges the gap between what I know to be true and what I am feeling is true.

It is no wonder that many of the prayers in Psalms were written to be accompanied by music. The circumstances of life disoriented the psalmists physically, emotionally, and spiritually. The reality of a sinful world, the actions of evildoers, or the depravity of their own hearts shook their lives and messed up the trajectory they were on. Through the psalms we are brought into their recovery or reorientation. The reorienting that takes place in them is both intellectual - they remind themselves of the truth of who God is and what He does - and emotional - they grieve openly and often do it with music.

The reorientation of the psalmists also does something else - it exposes and identifies the false gods of their hearts. As they are honest with their emotions, what they had been putting their hopes or happiness in is exposed. Emotions are often windows to our souls.

Like the dashboard of a car or the instrument panel of a plane they gauge what is happening inside me. Why am I feeling the way I do? Is my anxiety showing what else other than God I am putting my security in? Is my anger revealing frustration that my goals for success or expectations for comfort are not being fulfilled?

Recently I reflected on my life along the three basic needs for acceptance, security, and significance. I asked God to show me where I was seeking these outside of Him. I saw that good performance at work or softball made me feel significant. I saw that intimacy with my wife made me feel accepted. I saw that being organized helped me feel secure. In and of themselves there was nothing wrong with the activities. My heart, however, was skewed to look to them as gods, little idols. I wrote these on my whiteboard and alongside I listed the attributes of God that superseded them. Truth would triumph. I then spontaneously sang a song about it. Only in Christ am I fully accepted, significant, and secure.

Earlier this year I attended a workshop with key leaders of the Alliance. The first exercise was a fiasco for me. Distracted by my phone I missed the instructions so when it came time for the debrief my group hadn't done what we were supposed to do. I felt horrible and embarrassed. While the remaining 28 leaders gave their perfectly done feedback I wrestled in my soul. I began slipping into that insecure little shy boy who hid in the background. I caught myself and will never forget the words I said to myself, "No! I made a mistake. Everyone does. I don't need their approval. I am already accepted, secure, and significant in Christ. I don't have to go into conflict." Remarkably my emotions righted, my mind cleared, and I engaged in the rest of the workshop without insecurity.

I know I am in the right position when I am reminding myself of who God is, I am worshipping in music, and I am open to exposing the false gods that crop up.

POSITIONED FOR HIS POWER

Before I left for my first year at Bible college my small group at my Baptist church offered to pray for me. I told them I was afraid, but not for any of the usual reasons. I was afraid that I would trust in my own power. You see, getting A's was no big deal for me. Whether it was because of my great memory or my ability to know what the teacher wanted, I knew how to do well in school. I didn't want my college experience to be an extension of what I did in high school. I truly wanted to learn. I wanted to practice relying upon God's power.

After a few years in the pastorate it's easy to feel competent. You know how to be a pastor. Of course, the occasional crisis or new situations throw you for a loop, but for the most part ministry becomes something you know how to do. You chug along in a routine of sermon prep, visiting people, running meetings, and counseling folks. Even when a new challenge arises there's still the same operating system running in the background. More than one pastor has admitted to me, "I can do this in my sleep."

I am always reminded of Jesus' words, "Without me you can do nothing." (John 15:5) It's not that I cannot actually physically do something. I can mow my lawn (though I dislike to!). I can craft a 30 minute sermon. I can crunch numbers for a budget. I can do many things, but I cannot do anything of lasting spiritual value without the enablement and empowerment of Jesus.

How do I position myself for His power and not mine?

> *How do I position myself for His power not mine?*

I believe it begins with wanting it. Do I want more of the same or do I really want more of God? If I am satisfied with the status quo of where I am, or where my church is, of where my family is, then I doubt I will experience more power. If there is a holy discontent growing in me, if there's a hunger brewing, then I will experience more. Sometimes it takes an external crisis to get us to this point. Other times it's a wrestling match at the inner Peniel of our hearts.

I position myself by daily confessing my tendency to trust my own energy. I consciously and intentionally verbalize my dependency on Him for the day ahead. I acknowledge his gifting of me, but also admit that my gifting is not activated without His Spirit. I endeavor to maintain an attitude of reliance upon Him throughout the busy day. What I may do might not look any different but within me there's a huge difference.

For example, while in college I once wrapped up a research paper in timely fashion and walked away from the typewriter relieved that it was done. Suddenly it struck me that I had written the paper solely in my energy. I wrestled within, prayed, and then finally ripped up the paper. I started over and re-wrote it. It probably wasn't much different to the professor, but it was in my heart. The same has happened writing a sermon or ministering to people. Honestly there were times I didn't or couldn't start all over, but it is my desire to experience His power more than Bob's power.

Another way I position myself is by intentionally choosing to do things that are beyond what I feel competent for. I am not talking to those who get a rush out of risks and challenges, but to those who tend to take it safe. If I always do things that I can do myself, then it is harder for me to rely on someone else's strength. If I always minister out of my competency, then I miss out on experiencing God's power working through my weakness. For example, it's my strength to carefully research, plan out, and write out a sermon. The thought of stepping in front of people without a prepared message is a nightmare. Yet I have done just that and seen God's power at work. One time an entire outline popped in my mind when I needed it. It's not me, it's Him. And that gives me confidence.

Similarly I position myself by letting others do things that I think I can do better myself. It's my way of trusting God to work through someone else. It reinforces the truth that it doesn't depend on me.

For others, especially those who run headlong into challenges and want to get things done immediately, dependency is expressed in waiting, in yielding to others, or in extended times of prayerful inactivity. It is not a matter of correct behavior, but of heart attitude.

I live near Philadelphia, but still in the shadow of New York City. Frank Sinatra sings, "If I can make it there, I'll make it anywhere." It is all about success in New York. There is a huge emphasis placed on excellence, education, performance, and the bottom line. Not that there is anything inherently wrong in those things, but when our reliance, our dependency, our strength is measured the way our culture measures it, then we will find it difficult to truly position ourselves for His power. Sadly, I think many of us have unknowingly adopted that which we grew up in - a rational, academic, self-reliant, independent, performance based culture - so it's not natural for us to pursue the supernatural elements of our faith.

To do ministry, to be a minister, I need much more than my training, much more than my education, much more than self-help techniques, much more than my pragmatic Western mind can figure out. No, I need to tap into the divine within me, the supernatural power of God.

> *"His divine power has given us everything we need for a godly life through our knowledge of him who called us by his own glory and goodness." 2 Peter 1:3 NIV*

POSITIONED FOR HIS PEOPLE

I used to be shy, quiet, and extremely reserved.
I used to be paralyzed that I would be rejected.
I used to get social anxiety.

I used to fight with my wife before every party she forced me to attend. You can only imagine her surprise when for my 50th birthday I told her I wanted a big party. She was shocked! For the guy who thought a good time was being alone this was extremely abnormal. Over the previous 22 years, there was a dramatic shift in me away from the safe and secure patterns of my childhood toward the newness of God's community. As God was revealing more and more of His presence, person, and power to me, I was also experiencing the reality of Psalm 133

> Behold, how good and pleasant it is
>   when brothers dwell in unity!
> It is like the precious oil on the head,
>   running down on the beard,
> on the beard of Aaron,
>   running down on the collar of his robes!
> It is like the dew of Hermon,
>   which falls on the mountains of Zion!
> For there the Lord has commanded the blessing,
>   life forevermore.

I am introvert. I will always be an introvert. I will always need a break from people to recharge. Nonetheless, I enjoy being with people nowadays. Actually I NEED them. They have been God's instruments of encouragement and challenge in my life. They have been co-laborers in the gospel, confidants, prophetic or timely voices into my heart, or simply friends to share life with.

Granted, I have been disappointed, hurt, and betrayed by people. Those wounds cannot be glossed over, but the gospel keeps drawing me back to God's people. It's a community of flawed broken people, a community I enjoy. It's a community that has extended grace to me and allowed me the space to grow up. It is a people that has believed in me, released me, and supported me. It's a family that has cried with me. It a team that has served with me.

Last week only two pastors joined me at our quarterly prayer gathering. Normally I might be disappointed, but not this time. I consider these two men good friends. Not only have we served in the same area for twenty years, but we have journeyed together. Over the years we have prayed, cried, yelled, confessed, and played together. As a result, it was refreshing to spend three hours together worshipping, reflecting, and loving God together. It was a highlight to my month.

I really cannot say much more about this other that this - Avoid isolation. If I am alone, on my own, then insecurity, fear, and self-doubt will surely creep in. My self-talk needs to be countered by the actual talk of others. I need to laugh at myself, I need to be understood. I need to feel the embrace of the Father through others he sends my way.

Depressed? Don't pull away.
Discouraged? Don't just try harder.
Worn out? Don't keep plugging along.
Trapped in a sin? Don't hide it.
Feeling like a failure? Don't try to do it by yourself.
Get in the proper position for the relay. Get in community.

These four positions have been crucial to my journey. I saw them in the lives of Moses, Joshua, David, Jeremiah, and Paul, but moreover I experienced them to new levels throughout my own life. Experiencing the person, the power, the presence, and the people of God have crippled insecurity's hold over my life. I no longer have to strive to prove myself, to get people to like me, or to control things. I am free to be who God has made me.

FOR YOUR OWN REFLECTION:

1. How will you position yourself for His presence?

2. How will you position yourself for His person?

3. How will you position yourself for His power?

4. How will you position yourself for His people?

---

[1] - Tozer, A. W. (1982). *The Pursuit of God*. Camp Hill, PA: Christian Publications. Pg. 64.

CONCLUSION

Living in Christ is like playing a sport, but it's also not like playing a sport. We know that excelling at a sport involves training, repetition, and muscle memory so the body does things without thinking. Likewise, we need training, repetition, and habits in our spiritual journeys. However, it doesn't end there. We can't just shut off our minds and go into auto pilot. We're not just learning good behaviors. We are experiencing a Person.

Let me wrap up with one sports story that parallels my spiritual journey.

I have played slow pitch softball for decades. I love it and I do pretty well. Over the years I was invited to play on what are called tournament teams. These are really good teams made up of some of the best players in the area. Most of these men are a lot bigger than me. Their arms are wider than my neck! They are strong and can hit the ball a mile. I am a little guy who usually just hits singles. Every tournament with these big teammates I played horribly. One time, in particular, I popped up seven times to the infield; it was embarrassing. I couldn't play with these big guys because honestly I was intimidated and insecure. Subconsciously I was questioning, "How could I be on their team?"

Meanwhile there was an elite team in our area that was committed to using softball to reach prisoners - The Saints. They only chose the best players to visit prisons where they'd play extremely competitive softball and share Jesus. One day I got a call from the coach who had seen me play. He invited me to join them on a missions trip, a crusade to multiple prisons in Florida. Once again all the self-doubts and insecurities of my previous failures rushed into my mind. Nonetheless, I sensed God leading me to do this. I reluctantly accepted the invitation and went on the weeklong trip with a bunch of strangers who were bigger and, in my mind, better than me.

My first at bat came with the bases loaded. I hit a hard grounder that the pitcher grabbed and turned into a double play to end the inning. When I walked back, the coach pulled me aside and scolded me for going up the middle when the bases were loaded. Rather than take the normal route of withdrawing in insecurity and the fear of failure that I usually would take, I got alone, reminded myself of who I was in Christ, and that I didn't have to compare and prove my worth. The next at bat I hit a home run. Then that entire week I kept on getting hit after hit after hit.

It didn't end there. Our speaker got sick before he was supposed to preach and I had to sub on the spot with only thirty minutes to prepare. The response to the message God gave me on the spot was amazing.

Again it didn't end there. After one game I found myself surrounded by inmates wanting to talk because they were impressed with my performance; they wanted to hear my story. I was out of my element socializing with all these strangers ... and it didn't matter.

The morning we were leaving I wept as I sensed God saying. "See, when I tell you to do something, I will give you the power to do it. No more intimidation. No more insecurity. No more fear of failing. I am with you." At the end of the trip while we were waiting to pick up our luggage at the airport the coach came up to me. He shook my hand and thanked me for coming. He then said, "You can play with the big boys."

Until this day I still keep a Florida quarter on my desk to remind me of the truths God spoke to me over that softball trip. It was not about softball, not about batting averages, not about wins and losses, not about belonging to a team. No, it was about my heart experiencing freedom from insecurity by experiencing the presence, the person, the power, and the people of God.

Ministry is a lot more challenging than sports. It is far more dangerous for our souls. It is easy to get absorbed in what we are doing for God. It is convenient to settle for the poor substitute of acceptance, significance, and security that ministry provides. The calling placed on our lives is like that of Moses, David, Joshua, Jeremiah, and Paul. We will never be fully confident in ourselves. We are valuable coffee cups in which God has placed a magnificent treasure. Only in His Person, in His Presence, in His Power, and in His People will we find the confidence to lead.

Made in the USA
Middletown, DE
26 September 2017